# The Amish Circle Quilt

## 121 quilt block patterns that tell a story

Rosemary Youngs

Published by

**700 East State Street • Iola, WI 54990-0001**
**715-445-2214 • 888-457-2873**

Our toll-free number to place an order or obtain a free catalog is 800-258-0929.



Library of Congress Catalog Number: 2004098425

ISBN: 0-87349-891-7

Edited by Sarah Herman
Designed by Donna Mummery

Printed in the United States of America

# Dedication

It is with a heart full of love that I dedicate this book to my husband, Tom, my children, Stacey, Johnnathan, Amy and Jeffrey, and my first grandchild, Hailey Marie, and all of those that will follow.

# Acknowledgments

There are so many individuals that I would like to thank while I worked on preparations for this book. First of all, I would like to thank my family—my husband, Tom, my children, Johnnathan, Amy, Jeffrey, Stacey and her husband Micah and my granddaughter, Hailey Marie, for their loving support and encouragement.

To some of the best quilting friends a quilter could have: Judi Anderson, Gay Bomers, Barbara David, Bonnie Major, Barbara Perrin, Natalie Randall, Chris Yeager, Norma Zawistowski and Susan Zomberg. Thank you for rare and wonderful friendships. You truly are blessings in my life.

To those who spent a year in my class working on their own Amish Circle Letter Quilts at Grand Quilt: Judi Anderson, Gay Bomers, Barbara David, Norma DeBoer, Julie Dettloff, Megan Harding, Marian Heimler, Gretchen Houtman, JoAnn Ingersoll, Sandy Martinez, Marie McDonald, Linda Nikkel, Nell Renberg, Emma Steffy, Marlene Thompson, Nancy Vida, Loretta Weston, Sandy Ziebarth and Norma Zawistowski. Thank you for your support and encouragement and for your willingness to help produce samples for this book.

To my special friends, Pat Kuieck and Carol Schultz: Your friendships have always meant so much to me; dear friends you will always be.

To my acquisitions editor, Julie Stephani, and my editor, Sarah Herman, who believed in me and were willing to take a chance on a first-time author. To Krause Publications for their confidence and encouragement during the progress of this book.

To Tammy Finkler for her machine quilting expertise on the many projects she quilted for this book.

A heartfelt thank you to all the quilters I have met along my journey, whether we were in Shipshewana, Paducah, Beaver Island, the Attic Window Quilt Shop, or the West Michigan Quilters Guild. It would be impossible to list them all. Thank you especially to the girls that were so helpful starting my journey in quilt making: Cinda, LuAnn, Linda, Nancee and Sue.

Thank you to Jane Stickle, who in the 1860s designed her sampler quilt which has always been such a big inspiration to me. Thank you to those on the Internet list, especially Brenda Papadakis, for their belief and encouragement in pursuing the publishing of this book.

For the special pen pals who inspire me with their letters and photographs of their projects: Judy Day, JoAnn Fuhler and Maureen Baly.

I am indebted to the Amish communities, the women I have met and those I have observed, for their longstanding traditions and values of their faith and family in their communities. It is my hope that my book is an accurate portrayal of the traits and culture of the Amish people.

I would like to thank the Women's Bible Study of Trinity Reformed Church, which has enriched my life. Thank you for your encouragement, for believing in me and for your constant prayers. Most importantly, I would like to thank God, who always takes the pieces of my life, stitches them together and makes something beautiful.

# Table of Contents

# Preface

My fascination with the Amish people began about 15 years ago. I started spending some time each summer camping with my children in Amish communities. I am not sure why I became so intrigued with the simple and plain life of their people. I was first drawn in by the intense colors and simple geometric designs of their quilts. I soon began to observe their customs, everyday life, faith in God and closeness of the family unit.

It seems that I have come to learn so much about their people, but I still feel like an outsider looking at them through a glass window. I used to ride down the streets in the Amish buggy, trying to imagine what it would be like to live in the Amish family and community. As I passed the farms where the farmers were plowing, gardens blooming and laundry blowing in the wind, I wondered what it would be like to not be an outsider.

We no longer camp there during the summer. I now spend my time attending quilting retreats in their communities. Through what I have learned from my observations and conversations, I designed this quilt. There are 121 blocks in this quilt, each block with its own story. This story is told in the form of a circle letter, which is one of the many Amish customs.

A circle letter is the way people in different communities keep in contact with each other. A circle letter can circulate through a family, a group of friends or a group of teenagers. The first person to start the letter makes the list of who will receive the letter. When the second person receives the letter, she reads the first letter and then adds her own letter. Then it is sent to the third person who reads both letters and adds her own until everyone on the list has written a letter. Then it is sent back to the first person on the list who removes her first letter and adds a new one.

# How to Use This Book

You are about to embark on an exciting adventure. Not only will you learn about the Amish culture, but you will enjoy appliquéing and piecing together simple blocks. The book is divided into two sections. The first section covers general directions, fabric requirements and tools that are needed, as well as instructions to finish your quilt. The second section contains all 121 patterns and letters. After the letters, I include instructions for several projects using the various quilt blocks.

## Fabrics, Tools and Supplies

### Fabrics

Choosing fabrics is one of my favorite aspects of quilt-making. I always choose 100 percent cotton fabrics because I feel they work the best for needle-turn appliqué and piecing. The fabrics that you can choose for this quilt are endless. Whether you decide to choose a black background with vivid colors to create a dramatic effect, reproduction fabrics to create an antique look, or pastel fabrics to show the beauty, your quilt will become your own treasure to pass on to the next generation.

Do not be afraid to choose a rainbow of colors for this quilt, but make sure you choose a background fabric that does not distract from the other colors in the blocks and appliqué pieces. Selecting fabrics that have small-scale prints will be more effective than large-scale prints because the block is only 6" in size. It can also be fun to create a realistic effect using certain prints on your appliqué pieces to show texture and movement.

### Yardage requirements

6 yd. fabric for the background

6 yd. fabric for the lattice, border and binding

2½ yd. fabric for the cornerstones and inner border

Various fat quarters of coordinating fabrics for the appliqué and pieced blocks.

### Hand appliqué needles

Make sure that the needles for hand-appliqué are sharp and not quilting betweens. I found I have more control using a number 11 sharp. The higher the needle number, the longer the needle length and the easier it is to turn the edges under.

### Thread

I use 100 percent cotton, 50 weight thread in my sewing machine for foundation piecing and block piecing. The thread that I use for my needle embroidery is 60 weight cotton embroidery thread. I also used a 50 weight cotton embroidery thread for my buttonhole appliqué stitch.

### Pins

I use half inch appliqué, or sequin pins, to position my appliqué pieces on the background fabric.

### Rotary cutters, rulers and mats

I keep two different rotary cutters on hand. I use one to cut the fabric and the other to cut the fabrics that are sewn onto the foundation paper if I decide to foundation piece the block together.

### Scissors

Use a variety of scissors. I keep a pair of scissors handy just for paper cutting, a 4" pair of embroidery scissors to trim appliqué and thread and an 8" pair of scissors for cutting out the appliqué pieces and templates.

### Freezer paper

Freezer paper is a white paper that is adhesive when used with a hot iron and can be used for making your templates.

### Foundation paper

You can use foundation paper if you would like to foundation piece together some of the blocks, trace the block or the section of the block onto the paper and stich along the line accurately. Various brands of foundation paper are on the market and most of them work efficiently because they tear away from the fabric easily. I prefer to use foundation paper rather than interfacing because it tears away more easily.

## Using Templates for Appliqué and Piecing Together Your Blocks

Templates are patterns that you trace and cut that can be used whether you choose hand or machine appliqué and piecing. I use freezer paper not only because you can easily see through it to trace the template, but also because the template can be used several times. The more accurate you are in tracing your templates, the easier your block will fit together.

You will use the same technique whether you decide to sew your blocks by hand or machine.

**1.** Choose a block that you would like to work on and we will start by making the template. For an example, we will use the Christmas Cookies block.

**2.** Place a sheet of freezer paper over the pattern in the book; trace around all three shapes. Carefully cut out the template on the lines that you have drawn. Do not add any seam allowance.

**3.** Choose the fabrics that you would like to use for the three shapes. Set your iron to a no-steam setting and iron the freezer paper to the right side of the fabric.

**4.** Cut out all three shapes, adding a little less than ¼" seam allowance around all sides and parts of the template. If you are working on blocks where the pieces overlap one another, follow the same procedure, tracing around the whole template and then adding the seam allowance.

### Pieced block templates

**1.** Place your freezer paper over the drawing of the block in your book. Trace all the shapes onto the freezer paper adding ¼" seam allowance on all sides. To be more exact, use a pencil with thin lead for good, clear lines. It also helps to number the pieces to keep them in order.

**2.** Iron the freezer paper onto the right side of your fabric. Remember to set your iron to a no-steam setting. Cut out all of the shapes and assemble them as shown on the pattern.

## Adding Latice Strips

Cut the following sashing strips and cornerstones:
100 cornerstones (1½" square)
220 sashing strips (1½" x 6½")

**1.** Stitch the blocks into 11 rows of 11 blocks each with a sashing strip between each block. I used appliqué blocks alternately with my pieced blocks.

**2.** Stitch the rows together, matching the seams of the cornerstones with the seams of the lattice strips.

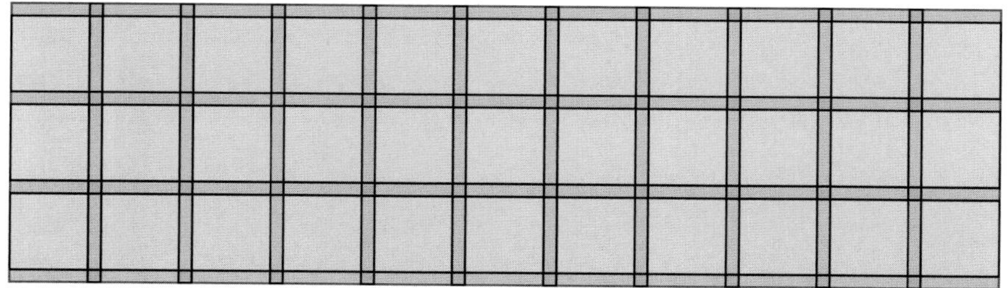

**3.** When all 11 rows are assembled together, the project should measure 76½" square.

## Borders

**1.** For the first small, inner border, which is going to be the cornerstone fabric, cut two strips 76½" x 1½" and two strips 78½" x 1½".

**2.** For the second inner border, cut two strips 78½" x 3½" and two strips 84½" x 3½".

**3.** For the outer border, cut two strips 84½" x 5½" and two strips 94½" x 5½".

**4.** Stitch the first two 76½" x 1½" border strips to the sides of the center of your quilt. Stitch using ¼" seam allowance, always pressing the seam allowances toward the center.

**5.** Add the two 78½" x 1½" strips to the top and bottom of your quilt.

**6.** For the second inner border, stitch the two 78½" x 3½" border strips to the top and bottom of your quilt.

**7.** Add the two 84½" x 3½" strips to the sides of your quilt.

**8.** To attach the outer border, stitch the two 84½" x 5½" border strips to the sides of your quilt.

**9.** Add the two 94½" x 5½" strips to the top and bottom of your quilt.

Join me in experiencing the everyday life of the Amish. Through the circle letter, I will guide you through the journey of 11 women who managed to maintain their friendship and record their lives. My wish for you, through making these quilt blocks and reading these letters, is that you will begin to learn more about the simple and plain life of the Amish people.

The story began 15 years ago when 11 girls graduated together from their eighth-grade class in a small Amish community in Indiana. They started a circle letter as teenagers and kept in touch with each other's lives through the letter. All of these women, at the start of the letter, are around 30 years of age and all are quilters. Some have moved to different communities, have married and are raising their families.

They have now decided that when they send their circle letter, they will enclose a 6" quilt block pertaining to something that happened in their lives during the week.

# Introduction

## Circle of Friends

### Rachel Yoder

Rachel is married to Samuel and they have six children: Lester and Lena (twins) are eight, Martha is seven, Jonas is four, Lyle is two and Kathryn is six months old. They are living on Samuel's parents' farm in a district in Indiana. Samuel's parents live in the Dawdy House.

### Lydiann Miller

Lydiann is married to Roy and they have four children: Clara is six, Katie is four, William is three and Amos is one. Roy owns his own small farm and runs a blacksmith shop out of his barn in a district in Pennsylvania.

### Martha Beiler

Martha is married to Eli and they have three children: Marlin is four, Vernon is three and Barbara is one. They live right down the street from Rachel and Samuel Yoder on a farm, taking care of their livestock.

### Rebecca Mast

Rebecca is married to Lyle and they have four children: Henry is six, Andy is four, Susie is two and Samuel is nine months old. They are living on a farm in a district in Ohio.

### Lavina Chupp

Lavina is married to Raymond and they have eight children: Noah is nine, Daniel is eight, Edith and Irene (twins) are six, Owen is five, Roseanna is three, Levi is two and Norman is 11 months old. They own a small apple orchard and vegetable farm and Raymond also works at a buggy and harness shop during the slow season in a district in Indiana.

### Edna Bontrager

Edna is married to Leroy and they have four children: Elvin is ten, Melvin is nine, Ruth is five and Naomi is three. They lived on Leroy's family farm and his parents live in the Dawdy House. They take care of the crops and a herd of dairy cows. Edna also does some quilting in her home for English customers in Indiana.

### Frieda Weaver

Frieda lives in Indiana. She is not married and teaches at the local schoolhouse. She lives on her parents' farm taking care of her ill parents.

### Lavern Esh

Lavern is married to Dan and they have three children: Dorothy is four, Joseph is three and Elis is two. They live on Lavern's parents' farm in Indiana and help them with the farming.

### Ida Hochstetler

Ida is married to Abe and they have five children: Mary is ten, Faye is eight, Eugene is five, Simon is four and John is three. They live on a small farm and Abe is a carpenter who runs a little furniture shop in Indiana.

### Regina Stolzfus

Regina is married to Freeman and they have six children: Martha is nine, Nathan is seven, Ivan is five, David is four, Katie is three and Lydiann is six months old. They live on a large alfalfa farm and hire local Amish to work on their farm in Ohio.

### Miriam Borkholder

Miriam's first husband died in a farming accident about three years ago and she has one child, Dale, who is six. She lives on her parents' farm to help out with the chores and works at a local quilt shop.

# Patterns and Letters

May 15

Dear Friends,

We have been so busy planning out our vegetable and flower gardens. Lena and Martha have been a big help to me while Lester is busy helping Samuel in the fields. School is out and the younger children enjoy having their brothers and sisters home all day. The weather is very pleasant, but we could use some rain for the plants that are starting to grow.

Have you realized that 15 years ago today was the day that we graduated from our eighth grade class? It has been so nice to keep in touch through this circle letter. I thought it would be nice that when we send out our circle letter, we each enclose a 6" quilt block depicting something that happened in our lives during that week. We are all quilters, so I thought it would be fun to share patterns.

The block I have enclosed represents our family picnic down by the pond. Last Saturday we packed picnic lunches and then met Samuel's family for a nice afternoon. There were 64 of us in attendance. The table was soon filled with food and freshly baked pies. When supper was finished, the men and boys started a game of baseball. Some of the women pulled out their handwork and enjoyed the time to visit. Just before dark, we sang a few of our favorite hymns and then headed for home.

Rachel

May 29

Dear Friends,

I enjoy reading all of your letters and really like Rachel's idea of sending along a quilt block. Living so far from all of you in Pennsylvania, I really look forward to reading the circle letter. I'm sitting in my kitchen looking out my window, as the children are playing in the yard. Amos is trying to do everything the older children do, while Clara seems to be really good at keeping him out of trouble.

We, too, have been busy getting our plants and flowers planted. The fruit trees are in bloom and it looks like we will have some delicious apples and pears later this season. The children are going to help me pick strawberries after lunch. William seems to eat more strawberries than he picks. We will have strawberry shortcake for dessert tonight.

Last night I finally finished quilting my Basket quilt. Clara and Katie enjoy sitting at the frame with me and always have the needles threaded when I need them. I used the last of my grandmother's leftover scraps from her scrap bag. The entire basket is set on a point with a green solid fabric. A red border surrounds it. I will bring the quilt to our reunion in August.

# 3. Collecting Eggs

June 12

Dear Friends,

On June 3rd, we were blessed with a new daughter who we named Nora. We think she looks exactly like her sister, Barbara. We have had so many friends and relatives visiting with us. Rachel and Miriam made Nora such a nice baby quilt. They used the log cabin pattern. They quilted it with a cable design.

Eli has been keeping busy in the field and with the animals. His brothers all came over on Saturday and helped him out. Little Marlin and Vernon are trying to be a big help by collecting the eggs from the chickens. They collected three baskets full and only managed to break one egg. They are trying to be just like Eli at their young age.

*Martha*

June 19

Dear Friends,

The weather here is so hot and humid and well over 90 degrees. It rained most of the night, so the fields received a nice watering. Regina's family came for supper last Sunday after church. We enjoyed each other's company and ended the night with a singing.

I have been picking beans and peas in the garden. The children seem to have so much fun with me in the garden. Since I have so many beans and peas now, I have been doing a lot of canning in the kitchen to catch up. Henry fell off of the fence yesterday. He needed a few stitches on his forehead, but he is back to his normal self today.

Tomorrow I am going to my Aunt Vonda's home for a quilting. We are working on a wedding quilt for one of her daughters. Her daughter was published to marry Enos Schmucker last Sunday at church. She has made a queen-size quilt using the Sunshine and Shadow pattern. She has planned for us to quilt diagonal lines in the squares and feathers in the borders.

Rebecca

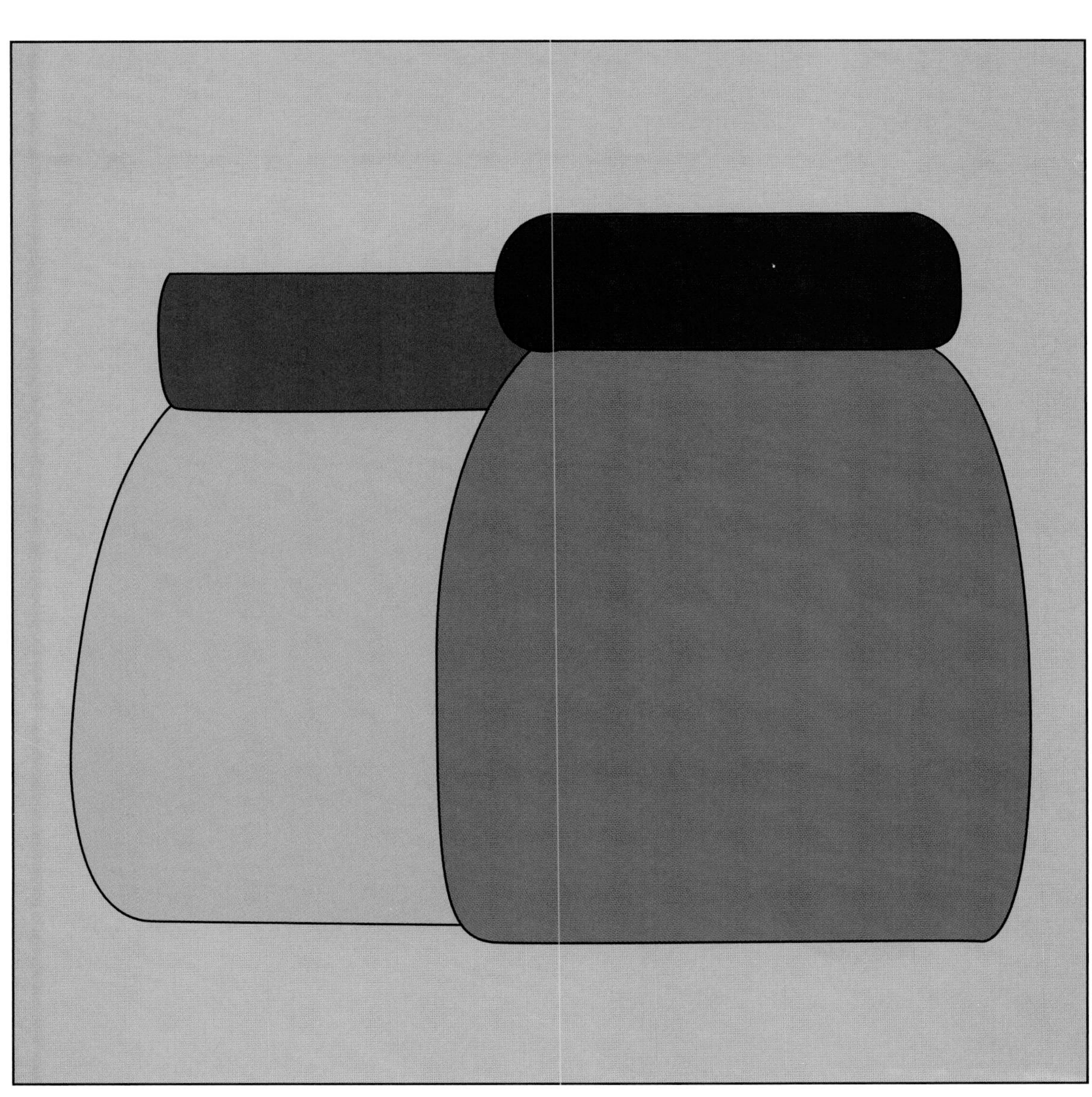

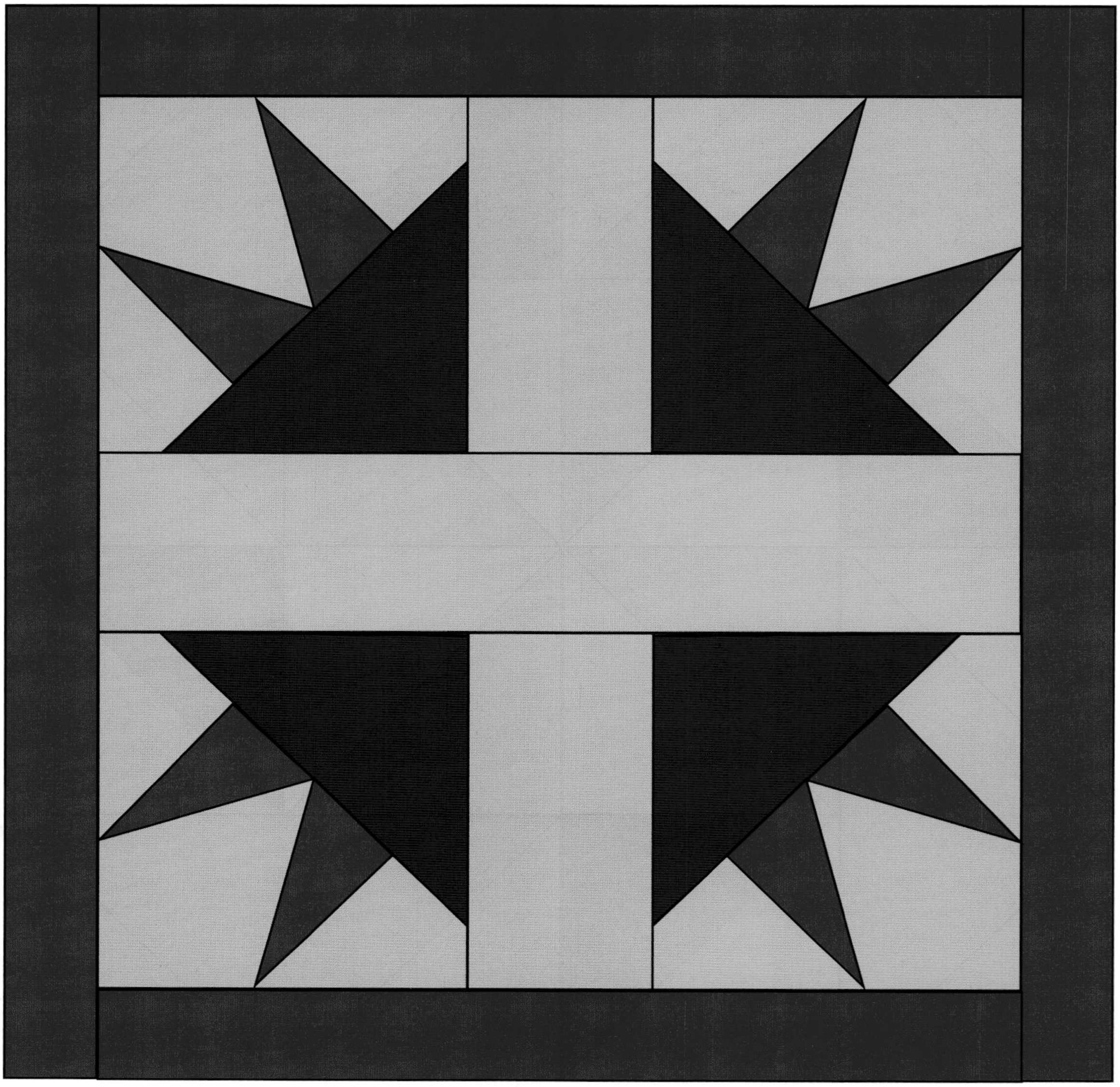

June 29

Dear Friends,

I was able to see Martha's new daughter, Nora, today. I took Levi and Norman with me, along with a couple of strawberry pies and three loaves of bread. The quilt that Rachel and Miriam made using Log Cabin blocks was just like the one they made for Norman.

Raymond has been very busy working at the buggy shop. The older children have been busy in the vegetable gardens and running the vegetable stand. Even little Norman tries to help. Irene and Edith are a big help when it comes to keeping him out of trouble. Last week he became entangled in the raspberry bushes. It just took a few scratches and he has stayed far away from them since.

Next week our family is heading down to Pennsylvania to visit Raymond's family. We're going to take a small vacation before the apples are ready for picking. We're also going to church with Roy and Lydiann on Sunday. I'm looking forward to visiting with her. Raymond has been working on the buggy and has put in a new battery so all of our reflectors and lamps will work. I have been canning some early sweet corn and doing plenty of baking.

July 14

Dear Friends,

I am sitting under the shade of our maple tree as I write this letter. It is very hot and sunny here today. I spent most of the day getting caught up on the laundry. It seemed to dry as soon as it was put on the line. I have been doing some mending and taking out some of the pleats in the girls' dresses. They seem to be growing so fast and I'm trying to get as much use out of their dresses as I can.

I have been quilting a Sunbonnet Sue quilt for one of my regular English customers. It is done in some really bright colors and she wants it to be heavily quilted. I will probably have this one in the frame until fall. I haven't had any time to work on any of my own quilting. This week I have been busy canning peaches and Leroy has been working on the second hay cutting.

I am sure most of you remember Marvin Miller. He graduated with us in the eighth grade and married Naomi Lambright. He was riding his bike to work and was killed. The funeral was on Friday with over 500 attending. She has six children to take care of and is living on Marvin's parents' farm.

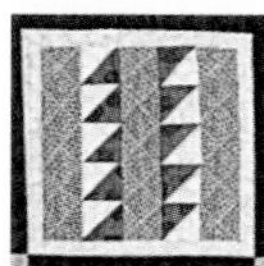

July 17

Dear Friends,

It is a beautiful summer morning, especially after the nice rain we had last night. Since the ground was so soft, I spent most of the morning weeding the garden. I really enjoyed my mail today. I received not only your circle letter, but also the circle letter from the teachers that I write to.

I have spent most of my summer so far taking care of Mom and Dad. Mom has been to the doctor's for cancer check-ups and radiation treatment. She is very uncomfortable. Dad's health seems to be declining. He is fighting bronchitis and is up most of the night coughing.

I'm looking forward to our reunion later this summer. It is so nice when our families get together. I know Miriam is really excited about having the gathering at her home. She already has her Pineapple quilt top finished for us to work on.

*Frieda*

8. Barn Raising

July 26

Dear Friends,

Our week has been full of activities. The Lord has truly blessed us with the addition of twins to our family. Emery and Karen were both born this past Tuesday. Our home has been busy. The children are doing fine and their brothers and sister are very helpful.

Raymond has been busy threshing the wheat. He is looking into buying some land adjacent to our farm. There seems to be such a large demand for farmland in our district.

The day before the twins were born, we spent the day at Lloyd Miller's, raising his family's new barn. They had a fire a couple of weeks ago. They didn't lose any of their livestock, but the barn was a total loss. Many families came to help. We set up a nice lunch for the men, and after they returned to work, we sat in the shade and quilted a red Feathered Star quilt for the Miller family. By suppertime, the quilt was finished. The men continued to work until dark. We ended the night singing some of our favorite hymns and then headed home. Some of the men will be returning this Saturday to finish.

Lavern

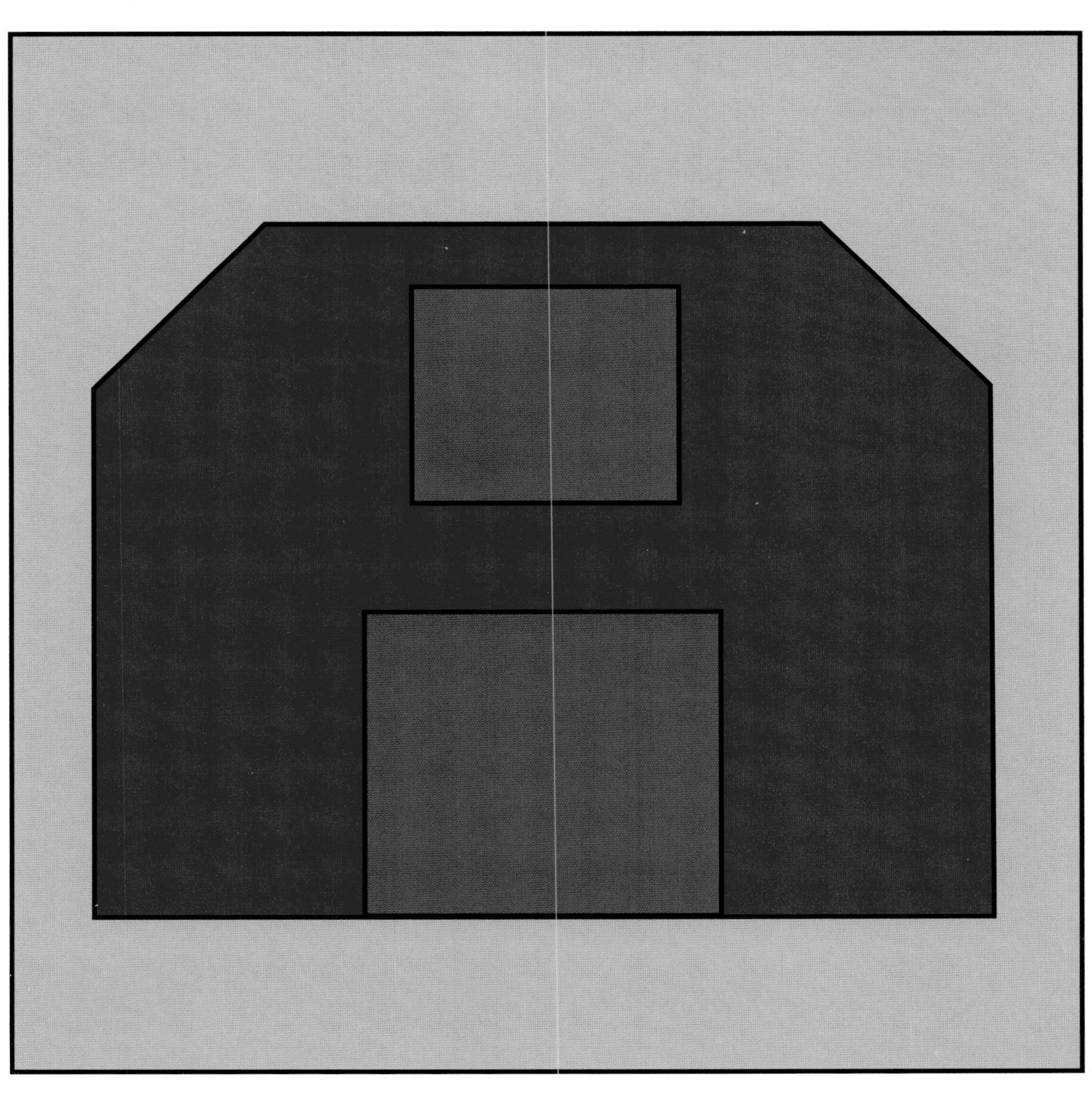

July 31

Dear Friends,

I just returned from visiting Lavern, Karen and Emery. They are doing very well. I took a couple of pies and some cherries with me. Her older children really enjoyed the cherries and I am sure that Dan will enjoy the pies. I also made each of the twins a Star baby quilt.

Once I was home, I began to get dinner ready. Mary and Faye have been trying some of Grandmother's old recipes. We had ham, potatoes, fresh green beans and bread. For dessert, we had homemade ice cream with cherries. After the dishes were done, I sat down with the girls and helped them work on their Nine-Patch squares. Their stitches are coming along very nicely. I am going to have them bring their tops with them to the reunion next month.

We hand-washed most of the comforters and quilts today and hung them on the line before I went to Lavern's home. An English woman stopped by and walked right into the backyard. The girls said that she was very demanding and wanted to buy a few of the quilts. Abe came in from the field and the woman then left. The girls were very relieved that their father was there.

*Ida*

August 6

Dear Friends,

Our family and Rebecca's family are getting ready for the trip to Indiana for the reunion. Freeman has hired some extra help to run the farm while we will be gone. I have been busy baking, canning and gathering my latest quilting projects to bring to share. The children are really excited about the trip. It will be so good to see each other again.

Martha has been doing some mending and sewing on my mother's treadle sewing machine. Her grandmother has also given her some old hexagons to piece together. She would like to make a Grandmother's Flower Garden quilt. All the hexagon pieces are made of wool from her scrap bag. My mother no longer quilts, but still enjoys cutting out pieces.

The sadness that I have to share, for those of you who haven't heard, is that both of Frieda's parents passed away last week. I have often wondered how people who don't understand God's ways could cope with this. Job 1:21.

Regina

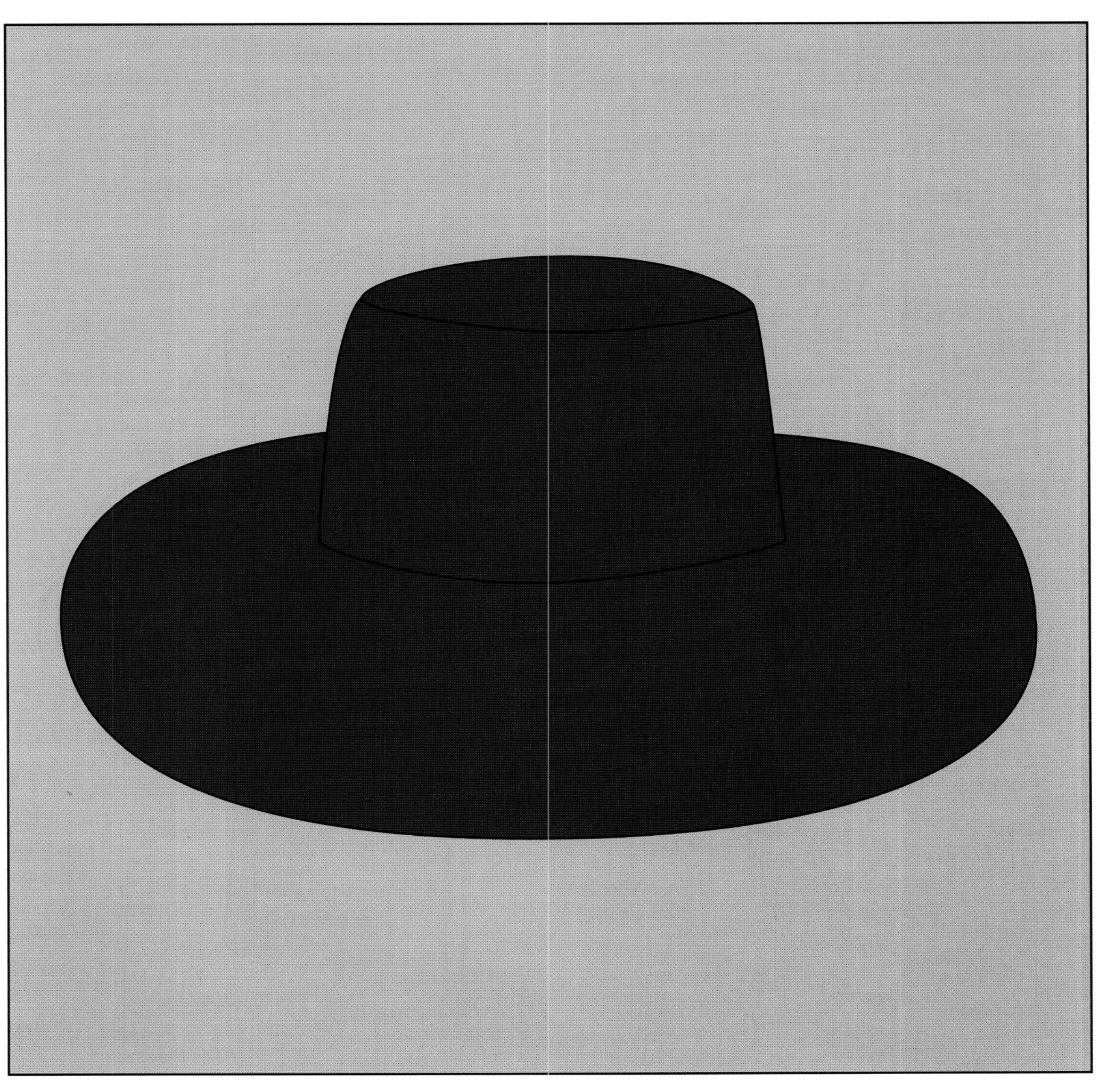

# 11. Pineapple Quilt

August 12

Dear Friends,

It's quiet here now as you are heading back home and I am writing my circle letter. Dale and I missed you as soon as you left. The reunion was a very good time and it was such a pleasure visiting with you. So much has happened since we were together last year. My how the children have grown in one year.

The picnics and singings were so enjoyable. It was also so nice to see each other's quilting projects. Your daughters have really learned a lot from each of you. It was interesting to see how some of the other children were taking such a big interest in our quilting. I can't believe that we finished quilting my Pineapple quilt top. I can't wait until next fall when we meet at Rachel's.

I will close for now. Dale and I are headed outside to help my parents with some chores. It is the time of the year when my father has us help him trim the grapevines. Tonight I think I will begin to bind my Pineapple quilt.

August 21

Dear Friends,

It was such a pleasure to visit with you all two weeks ago. The quilts that you brought to the reunion have really inspired me. Lydiann, I really would like to start a Basket quilt like the one you made using scraps from your grandmother. I have a couple scrap bags in the attic that I would like to use.

Samuel's mother and I spent most of the afternoon baking apple and peach pies. The kitchen smelled so good. We then prepared a big supper and my brother and his family came to visit. There was a nice summer breeze, so we all sat on the porch and enjoyed our pie and ice cream.

I have been working with Martha and Lena on sewing their Nine-Patch quilts together. Tomorrow I'm taking the girls with me to a relief quilting that is to be held at Fannie King's home. They are very good at watching the children and helping prepare the lunch.

Rachel

# 13. Diamond in the Square

September 1

Dear Friends,

I am enjoying not only the circle letter, but also the blocks that we have been sending with it. Rachel, I really enjoyed tracing your last block of pie. I hope we continue to exchange the blocks. Maybe someday we will have enough blocks to put together a quilt. We will then have a quilt that contains memories for all of us.

Roy has been spending most of his time in the blacksmith shop. I always sell a lot more of my jams and jellies when he is busy. This week I'll be in the kitchen canning mostly apple jelly because the apples are ripe. The children really enjoy when the apples are ready because they know there will be plenty of apple butter and fresh baked bread to go with them.

I have a Diamond in the Square quilt in my frame now. I'm having a quilting here next week to work on it. My youngest sister is to marry in about two weeks. She was published to marry Joseph Kauffman this past Sunday in church.

Lydiann

# 14. Watermelon Wagon

September 8

Dear Friends,

It is a nice and sunny 70-degree fall day here. Little Nora is trying so hard to crawl already. She really enjoys when the other children play with her. Sometimes Marlin and Vernon can really get her laughing.

Today we went to the farmers' market to sell some watermelons. It was so much fun to watch the boys try to load the watermelons into the wagon. We sold all the watermelons and the children used the wagon to pull each other home.

There was a buggy accident on the main road on the way home. We could hear the sirens. We have heard that everyone is all right, but that they were taking two of the younger children to the hospital. We don't know the family. They are from another district in Indiana.

*Martha*

# 15. Comfort

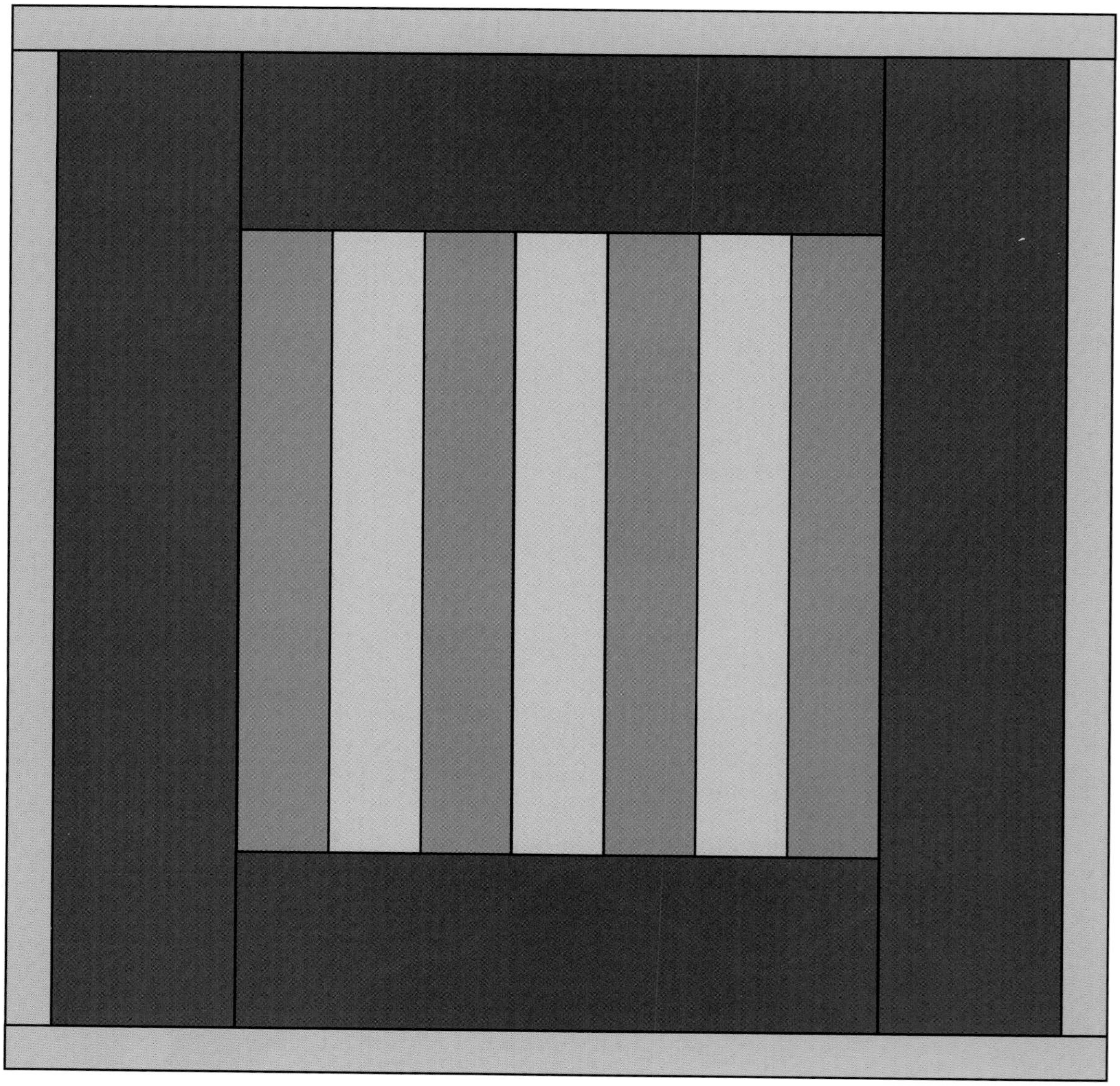

September 29

Dear Friends,

I will try to write about the tragedy that came into our lives two weeks ago. I know that most of you attended the funeral of our daughter, who we named Lucy. She was stillborn on September 15th. God's ways are always best. The funeral was held in our barn, with about 300 in attendance. The comfort we received from our friends and neighbors was overwhelming. Neighbors are still coming over for visits and are helping out with the chores.

We know that this is God's will and we have found a lot of comfort from Psalm 91. Thank you for all your support to help ease our pain. We have felt so much support from family and friends.

*Rebecca*

October 9

Dear Friends,

It is a beautiful fall day with temperatures around 70 degrees. Raymond has been very busy with Noah and Daniel in the apple orchards. We have been selling apples by the bushel all day long.

A horse kicked our neighbor, Morris Schrock, today. His mother came over running and sent Raymond running down to the corner to use the phone booth to call for help. They have returned home and he is doing much better, but will be laid up for a while. We took them dinner and Raymond helped milk their dairy cows. I have enclosed his address. I thought it would be nice if we could send him some cards in the mail. Morris is only 8 years old and would really enjoy receiving some mail.

I am enjoying the cool weather and it seems like I am finding a little more time for my quilting. I have been working on a Double Nine-Patch quilt. I have two blocks yet to hand piece and then the top will be ready for the frame. It is made using some purple, blue and green fabric that I had left over from my last project.

Lavina

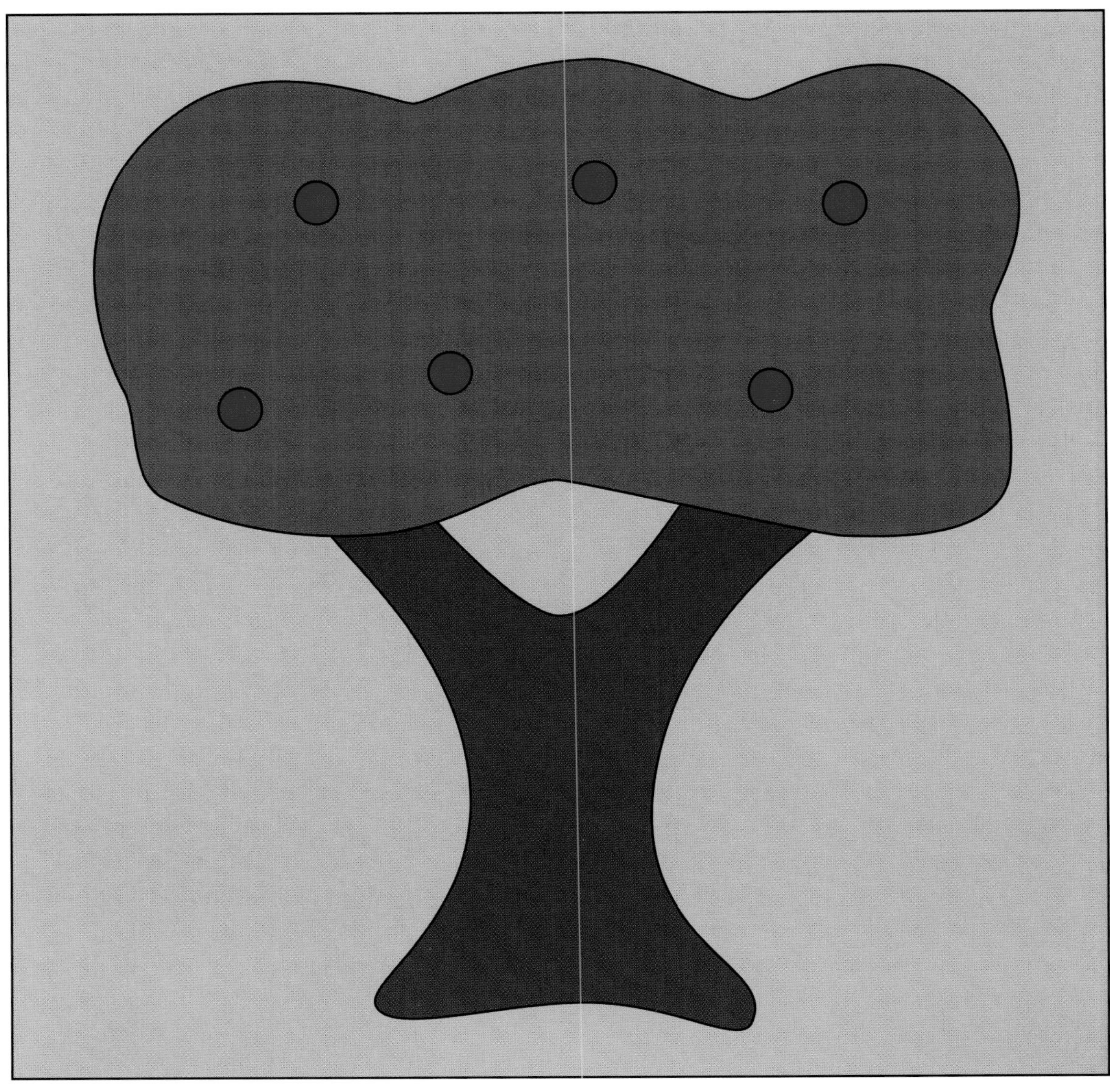

# 17. Maple Leaf

October 19

Dear Friends,

Our family has been blessed with a new son, born on October 11th, who we named Lloyd. He is such a good baby. He hardly ever cries. He naps more than our other children ever have. We have had so many visitors and family members helping us out this week. On Sunday we had over 30 visitors to our home.

I just finished quilting a Maple Leaf quilt for one of my English customers. It was fun to quilt the leaves as I would watch the leaves fall out of the trees in our yard. I'm not going to be working on any other quilts for a couple of months.

I'm really glad that Leroy's parents are living in the Dawdy House. They are both in good health and are a big help on the farm. His father is always helping Leroy guide the team of horses in the field. Another one of his favorite chores is taking care of the livestock. Leroy's mother is always helping me in the kitchen and with my quilting.

October 26

Dear Friends,

We have been having some nice weather, but with cooler nights. I have visited with Edna and her new son, Lloyd. I made Lloyd a small baby quilt using the scraps that I had left over from the Pineapple quilt that you all helped me quilt at the reunion.

The good news that I have to share is that I married Marvin Hershberger last week. He is a widower and has three children. Timothy is six, Joseph is five and Edith is only three. It's been a busy week and I have enjoyed getting to know the children. I will be moving from my parents' farm to Marvin's home. The other exciting news is that Rebecca and her family are going to be buying my parents' farm and moving back from Ohio to our district.

Last night the families of my school children held a supper and singing at the school for me. They recited a special prayer in German for me. I will no longer be teaching. One of my former students is going to replace me.

*Frieda*

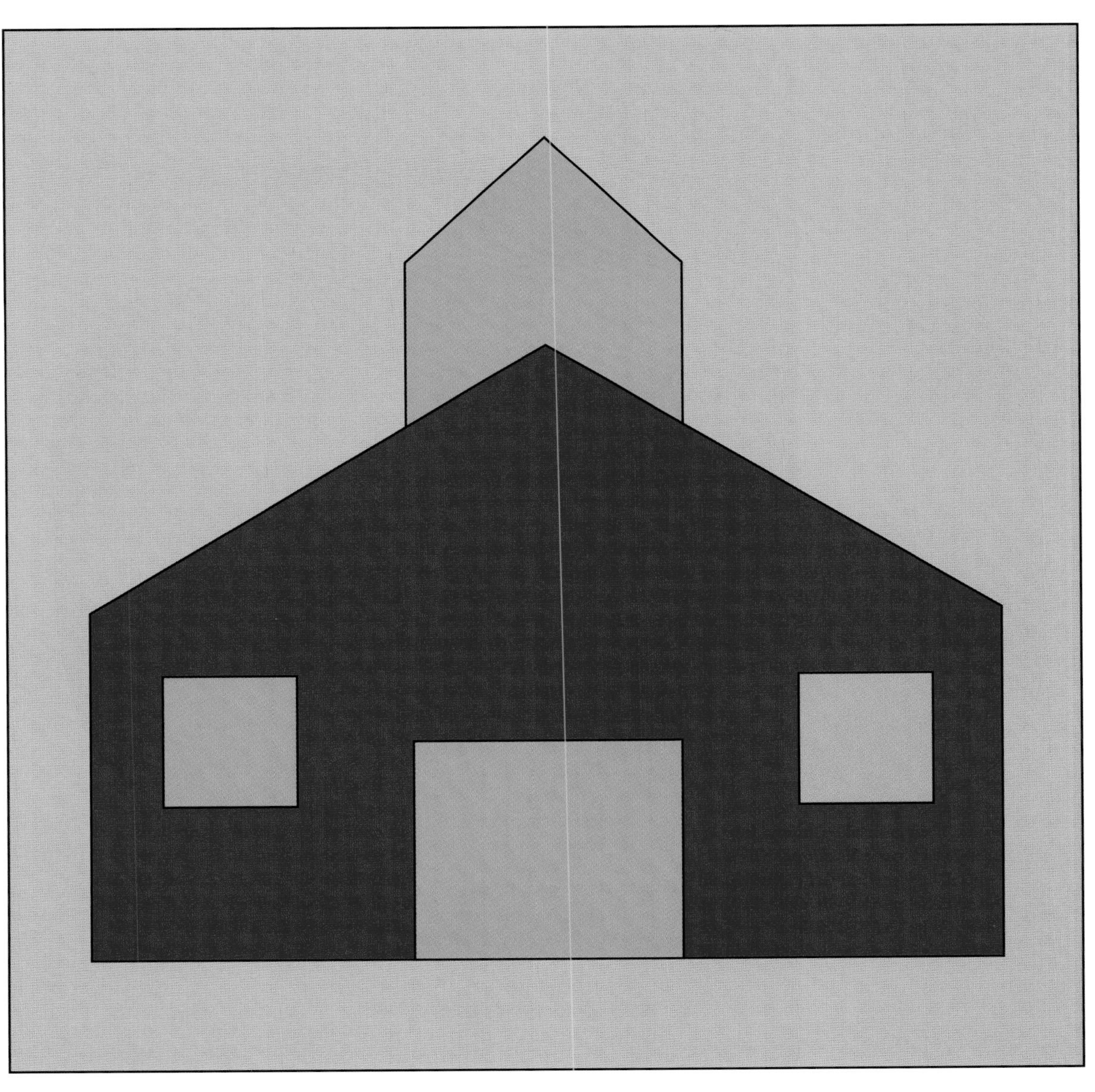

# 19. Surprise Quilting

November 5

Dear Friends,

The days seem to be a lot cooler. The twins are doing really well and growing very fast. We're all going to visit Frieda's family for supper tonight. I have baked some apple pies and pumpkin bars to take along.

I was really surprised yesterday. There was a knock on the door when I was working in the kitchen. Some of the ladies from our church district surprised me and brought lunch. They spent the rest of that afternoon quilting my Star quilt that was on the frame. They left right before supper and my quilt was finished.

Dan has been very busy on the farm pruning the trees this week. He did take some time on Friday and went to the auction to buy a new cultivator for the draft horses to pull. He also came home with three bags of fabric scraps for me. I am going to hand piece an Ocean waves quilt when I get the scraps sorted out.

Lavern

November 11

Dear Friends,

The girls spent yesterday gathering the pumpkins that were left in the fields. We spent the day baking pumpkin pie and bread. Today we spent most of the day helping Rebecca and her family move into their new home. Some of you attended and it was so good to see all of you. The men managed to get all the furniture moved into the home and were mighty hungry. We ended the night with a supper and a singing.

Abe presented Mary and Faye last week with small wooden quilt frames. They are going to try quilting their next quilts in their frames instead of using a hoop. He made them in his furniture shop and they were a complete surprise to the girls. Now that the weather is getting cooler, Abe will be spending more time in his furniture shop than in the fields.

I have just put a Fan quilt top that my mother never finished into the frame. She made it primarily out of wool and intermingled a few cotton scraps. She said it was a project that she and my grandmother worked on together. I thought it would be nice if I had Mary and Faye help me quilt it. I'm going to let them get started on some of the straight lines because that will be easier for them to quilt. I think that since my mother gave this to me, it would be nice if it was passed down to the next generation.

*Ida*

# 21. Winds and Snow

November 26

Dear Friends,

It has been unusually cold. We had some light snow and high winds down here in Ohio. I had to hang the laundry in the kitchen by the stove to dry today.

Rebecca, we hope that you are settled and that things are going well in your new home. Our family misses you very much. The children already want to come for a visit. I'm also very happy for you, Frieda. I can't wait to meet your new family. Freeman is talking about taking a trip up to visit with his brother during January since it is slow time on the farm. A few of our Amish neighbors have agreed to take care of our livestock.

The children and I are going to spend the day cleaning our home. Some ladies from our church district are coming over tomorrow to help wash the walls. We also have some baking to do because church will be held here this Sunday. There are enough families in our church district that we only hold church once a year in our home.

Martha has been working on piecing together her hexagons. My mother has been helping her. When the top is finished, we will have a quilting day for some of our family members.

*Regina*

# 22. Quilt Shop

December 15

Dear Friends,

We had a quilting here last week. Martha, Edna and Frieda were in attendance. We worked on quilting a small Nine-Patch quilt for Rachel's new son. They then helped me baste my Log Cabin quilt and put it in the frame.

I have been very busy at the quilt shop. The weather has been warmer than usual and it seems to have brought more customers out this week. I enjoy working there in the morning while Dale is in school. Dale and I will be traveling by train next week to visit my sister for a few days. She just gave birth to her ninth child, Jonas, which makes five boys and four girls.

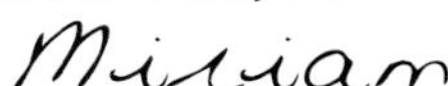

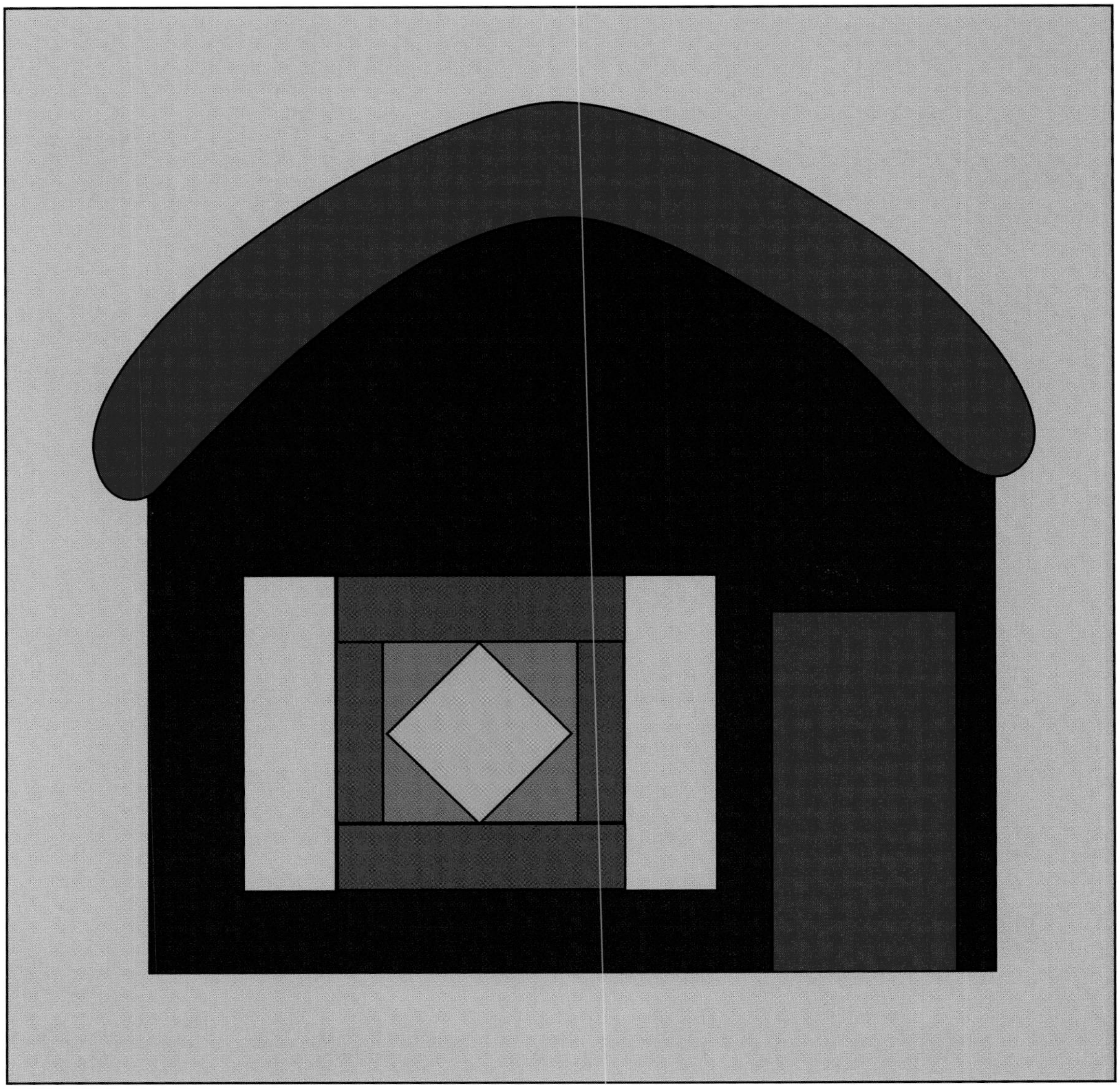

# 23. Nine-Patch Quilt

December 28

Dear Friends,

Two weeks ago, on December 10th, we added a son to our family. We chose the name Henry. The children are so excited about the new baby and all the company we have had coming and going in the last two weeks.

The children held a really nice Christmas Eve program at school. One of the skits they performed was spoken in Pennsylvania Dutch. Their grandparents really seemed to enjoy that part of the program. On Christmas Day, we had a Christmas dinner here with 46 in attendance. On the second day of Christmas, we went to my sister's home for dinner and a singing.

The weather here has been very cold and icy. Yesterday I was surprised to see Miriam and Martha standing in my kitchen with the Nine-Patch quilt that they made for Henry. They also brought fresh bread, apple pie and some vegetable soup.

I have been working on my Basket quilt with the old scraps. Martha and Lena have been using some of the scraps in their Nine-Patch quilts. We enjoy our time at night when we sit around the oil lamp and hand piece our blocks together.

*Rachel*

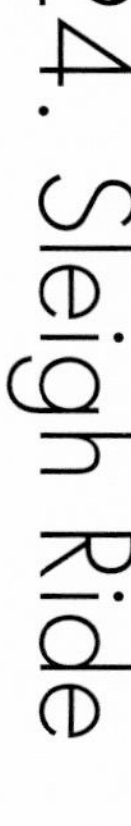


January 5

Dear Friends,

The weather here has been bitterly cold. Yesterday Roy took Clara to school in the sleigh. The other children went along for the ride. They all came home with really red, rosy cheeks because the temperatures were well below zero. They all huddled around the stove when they returned home. The hot chocolate and fresh doughnuts that were waiting for them brought smiles to their faces.

It will be a very busy week at our house. Church will be held here this Sunday. Roy and I always have help from our neighbors in getting ready. Some of the men are coming here tomorrow to help set up the benches. The women are going to help me clean and prepare a light lunch. We have about 90 in our church district, but the weather might keep some young families at home.

I went to a quilting frolic two weeks ago with 32 of us in attendance. We spent the day quilting on two quilts for the school benefit. One of the quilts was an unusual Sawtooth Diamond and the other quilt was a traditional Sunshine and Shadow quilt. The families came later in the day. We ended the night with a supper and a singing. It was a nice evening and made me think of the last time all of us were sitting around the quilt frame at our reunion. I'm so glad that we have kept up our circle letter.

Lydiann

# 25. Roman Stripes

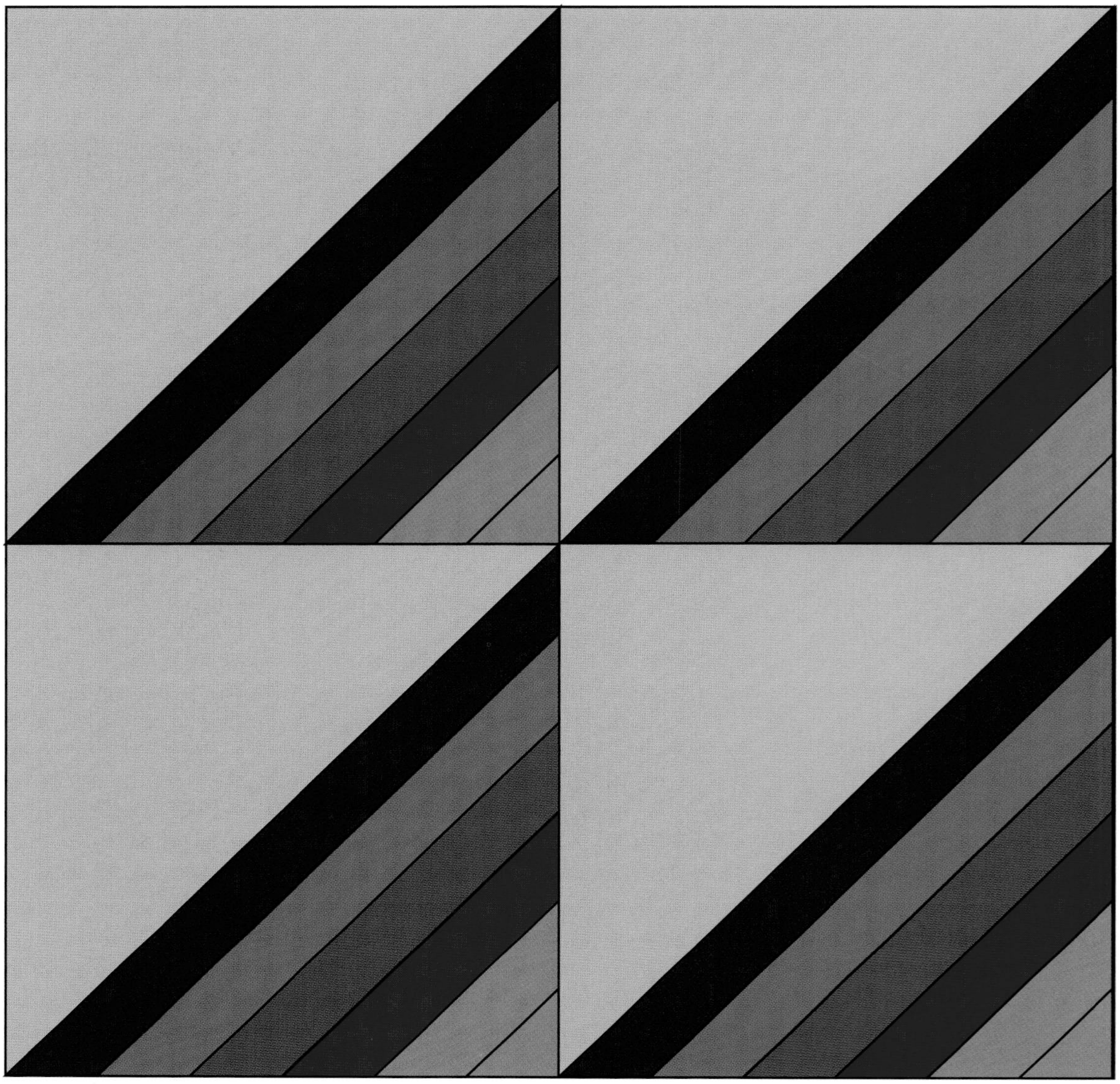

January 16

Dear Friends,

Eli has taken Marlin and Vernon sledding today. Barbara and Nora are playing quietly, so I have some time to catch up on what has been going on in your lives. I have begun to work on some of the patterns that we have been sending each other. Today I have enclosed a Roman Stripes pattern because that is the quilt that I have in the frame right now. It has been difficult for me to work on this particular quilt. It was the last top my mother finished before she passed away and is made with some of our old dresses and clothes that our family had as children. It holds many memories.

Regina and her family arrived safely from Ohio. They are visiting with our family and some of their relatives in our district. Last night Rachel's and Frieda's families were here visiting, too. Edna's family had planned to join us, but her family has come down with the flu. After dinner, we sat around the quilt frame and worked on my mother's quilt. We had some apple pie and ice cream for dessert and then everyone headed for home.

# 26. Butchering the Pigs

January 25

Dear Friends,

Our family has settled well into Frieda's parents' home. Lyle is looking forward to the warmer weather so he can get started working in the fields. He went to a livestock auction last week and bought 12 new dairy cows and 200 chickens.

It is so good to be back in our district where our family and friends live. The children have adjusted well and it is hard to believe that Henry is going to the same school as I did.

We spent this past Friday with two other families. It was time to butcher the pigs to replenish our supplies of canned pork. The men spent most of their time working in the barn while the women were in the kitchen watching the children and canning the pork. We all had a nice supper together of fresh sausage, potatoes, corn and fresh baked bread with apple butter. Next week we're going to butcher the chickens and make some chicken soup.

Rebecca

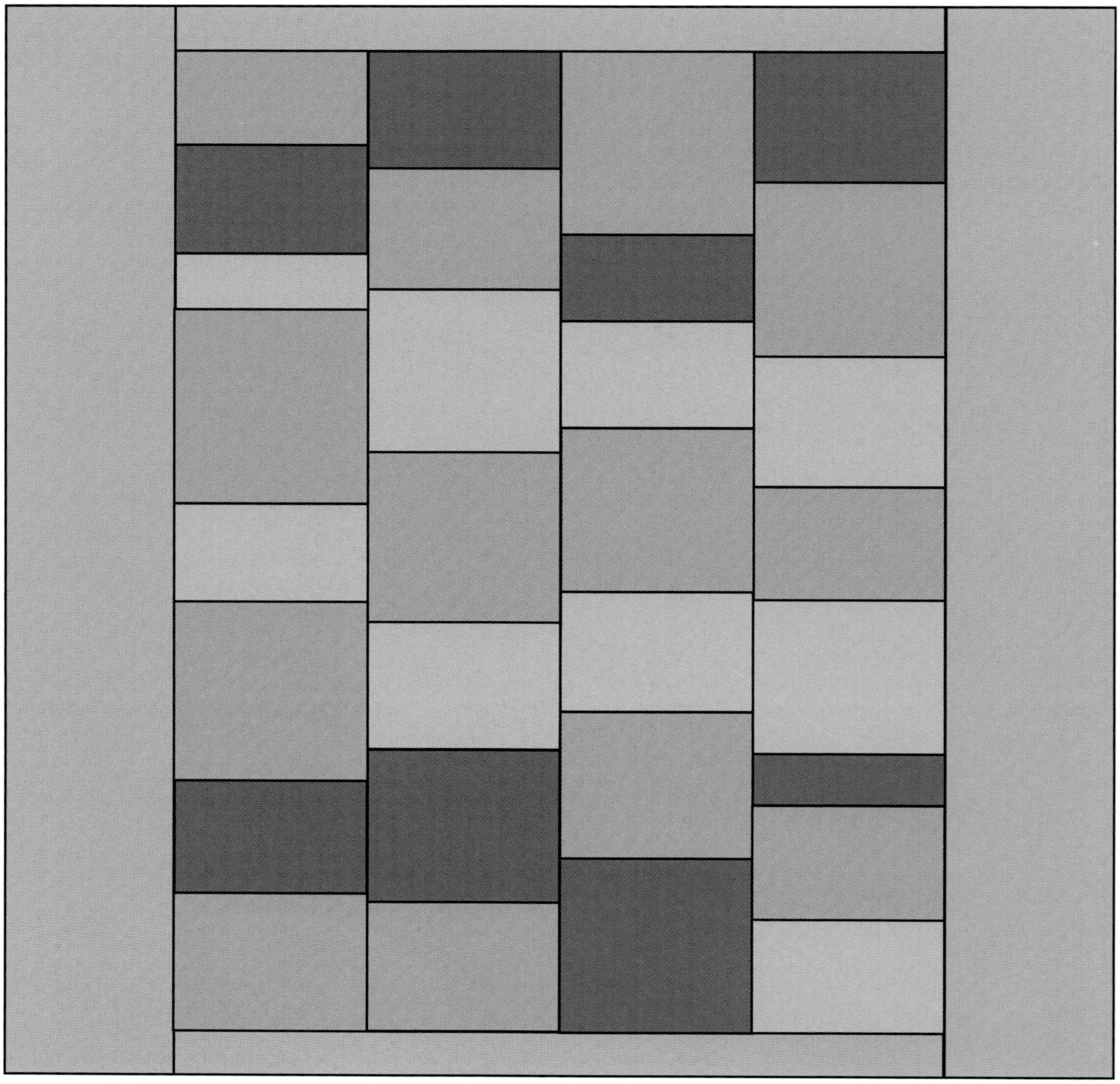

# 27. Ice Harvesting

February 1

Dear Friends,

Last week we had our ninth child, a little boy who we named Reuben. Raymond hired a girl to help me out with the children and the household chores. She is a very good worker. Her name is Anna Wengerd and is the daughter of Mervin and Fannie. Anna has been sitting down at the quilt frame when the children are in bed. She has also been helping Mary and Faye with their quilting projects. She has been showing them her piecing techniques.

Raymond's father and brothers have been helping him cut ice blocks and are filling up the icehouse this week. Even the children have been trying to haul ice blocks on their sleds. It is so nice to have his family here visiting with us.

# 28. Box Social

February 9

Dear Friends,

We have just returned from the doctor's and the news was not good. We have been going through some testing with Lloyd. He is five months-old now and spends most of the day sleeping. They have found a tumor on his brain and it is inoperable. All we can do for him right now is keep him comfortable. We know that children are a gift from God and even though it will be hard to let go, we know God gives us our children to care for as long as he sees best. Romans 12:2.

We went to the schoolhouse yesterday for a box social for the youth to raise money to help pay for some of Lloyd's hospital expenses. It was so nice to see how the girls decorated their boxes. We enjoyed watching the boys bid on the meals that were inside. We had to laugh when Wayne Miller bid on his own sister's box, not knowing it was hers. There were approximately 60 youths in attendance and the event raised $321.

Edna

# 29. Buggy Accident

February 20

Dear Friends,

Last Sunday as Rachel's family was heading to church, there was a terrible buggy accident. The road conditions were icy and a car slid into their buggy. The horse started to run uncontrollably and tipped the buggy over. Most of the family was thrown from the buggy. Martha has a broken arm and Jonas needed some stitches. Rachel has a broken arm and her husband, Samuel, broke both of his legs.

Samuel will be in a wheelchair for about six weeks. Our family, along with other families and neighbors, will all be helping with the chores on the farm. Samuel's parents are living in the Dawdy House and they will be a big help taking care of the family.

On Wednesday, Edna's son, Lloyd, passed away and the funeral was held on Friday. This will be a week we will not forget. We know that this is God's will and that He let this happen for a purpose. We also know we must not question God's plans.

*Frieda*

# 30. First Robin

March 9

Dear Friends,

We drove over to Rachel's this past Saturday. Dan worked with the neighbors on the farm and I helped Rachel and her family in the kitchen. We had a really nice lunch together and it was so nice for so many to be down helping. The men really accomplished a lot of the chores that needed to be done and have set up a schedule to help milk the cows and take care of the other livestock.

The day had rather pleasant weather to get some things accomplished. The children were playing outside and saw the first robin of the season. We're hoping warmer weather is around the corner. Some of the snow is beginning to melt and it will soon be time for us to be planting our flower and vegetable gardens.

I have finished hand piecing my Ocean Waves quilt. It will be big enough to fit on a queen-size bed. I'm going to work on putting it in the frame tomorrow night. I'm going to do outline quilting in the triangles, so it should be finished in a couple of months. I will bring it to the reunion with me in August.

Lavern

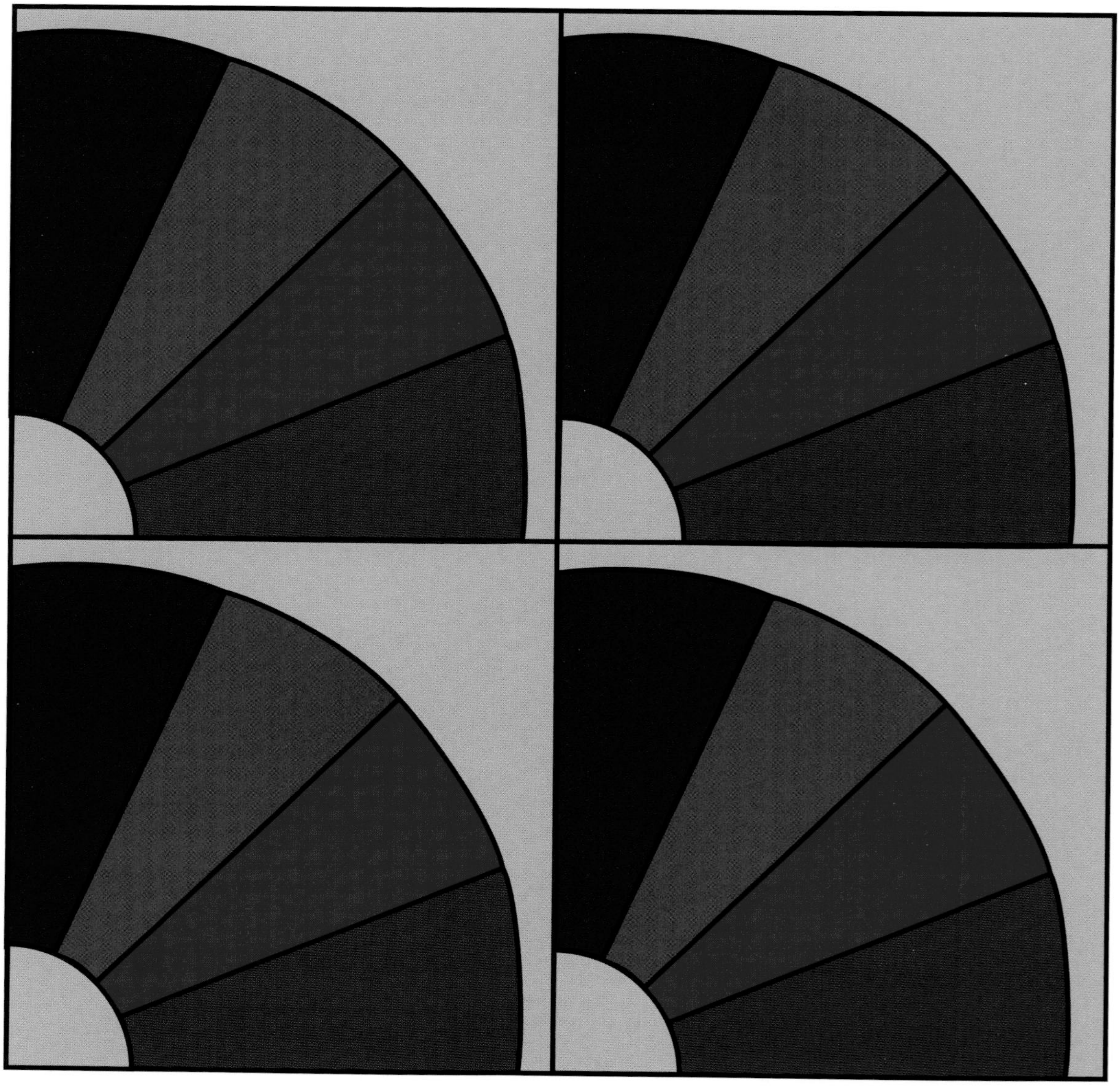

# 31. Wool Fan Quilt

March 19

Dear Friends,

The snow has melted and the weather here is getting warmer everyday. If you haven't heard, on March 16th we were blessed with a healthy little daughter who we named Nettie. She is a very good baby and the girls are having a lot of fun helping me take care of her. Abe made her a new wooden cradle in his furniture shop because we gave ours to one of his sisters to use.

I finally finished my Fan quilt top that my mother gave me. It had been in the frame for about four months. I used over 500 yards of thread and found that quilting through the wool was not as easy as going through cotton. I am hand piecing some of the blocks that we have been exchanging. When I look at the blocks, they remind me of the events in your lives that you designed the blocks for. I'm sending the pattern of my Fan quilt, with hopes that some of you get the chance to make your own block.

Tomorrow we are having a frolic here to help build an addition to Abe's furniture shop. He has been really busy lately and needs a little more room to store some of his finished work. Quite a few of the men folk are going to be here, so it will probably be finished in no time at all.

*Ida*

# 32. Spring Flowers

March 26

Dear Friends,

The sun is shining and the weather is in the 70s. We took a walk today down to the lake to have a picnic. We met two other families and had a wonderful lunch. We were surprised to see flowers blooming in the field after such a hard winter.

One of my neighbors brought some comforters for us to sit on. When we were done with lunch, we helped her tie them. The children joined in and in no time the comforters were tied. It was a lot of fun. I have never tied a comforter in the grass. After that, we watched the men folk and the children play a game of baseball. Freeman sprained his ankle and had to hobble all the way home.

I started to work on an Eight-Pointed Star quilt. The quilt is composed of only two colors and the stars are purple, set on a light background. Everything seems to be going well and the children seem to be growing so fast. I can't wait until you can see them at our next reunion.

*Regina*

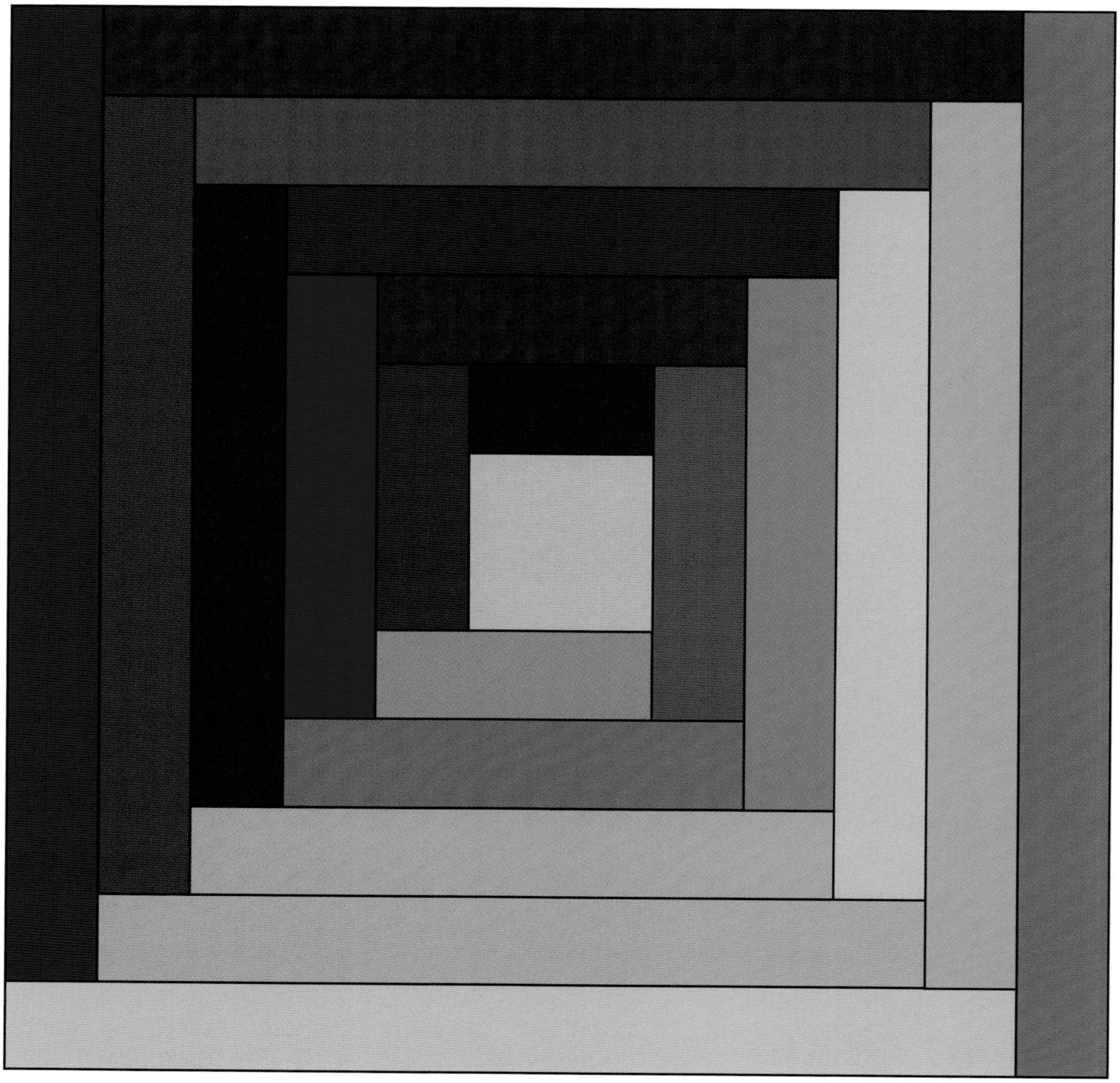

# 33. Log Cabin Quilt

April 9

Dear Friends,

Well, my Log Cabin quilt is finally finished and just in time, as I will be marrying Daniel Schlabach. He is a widower and has four children; Jacob is nine, Andy is seven, Mary is six and Katie is four. Dale and I are really looking forward to becoming part of their family. Daniel is very busy taking care of his farm and being the bishop of his district. We will be moving into his home after we are married in two weeks. He is the bishop of the district that Lavern lives in, so I will not be moving very far away.

I will not be working at the quilt shop, but I am looking forward to taking care of Daniel and the children. Daniel also has a large vegetable and flower garden and a good deal of chickens to care for. His children really enjoy doing farm chores and Dale can't wait to learn more about farming.

# 34. Apple and Apricot Blossoms

April 15

Dear Friends,

Things seem to be going much better since the accident. Samuel is slowly healing, but is still using his wheelchair. The children seem to be fine, but are frightened now to ride in the buggy. I have been trying to do as many of the chores as I can. We had so much help from our family and friends and most importantly, we depend on God to help us get through each and every day.

The children are helping me plant some flowers along with some rhubarb, lettuce and beans. The apricot and apple trees are blossoming with big white and pink flowers.

Last Friday we had a work frolic on the farm. So many family and friends came out to help. Even a few of our English neighbors were there. As the men worked, the women made me a Friendship quilt that we put in the frame and quilted. We set up some tables outside and had a supper of chicken, ham, potatoes, vegetables and ice cream for dessert. There were 68 in attendance. We ended the night singing our favorite hymns.

*Rachel*

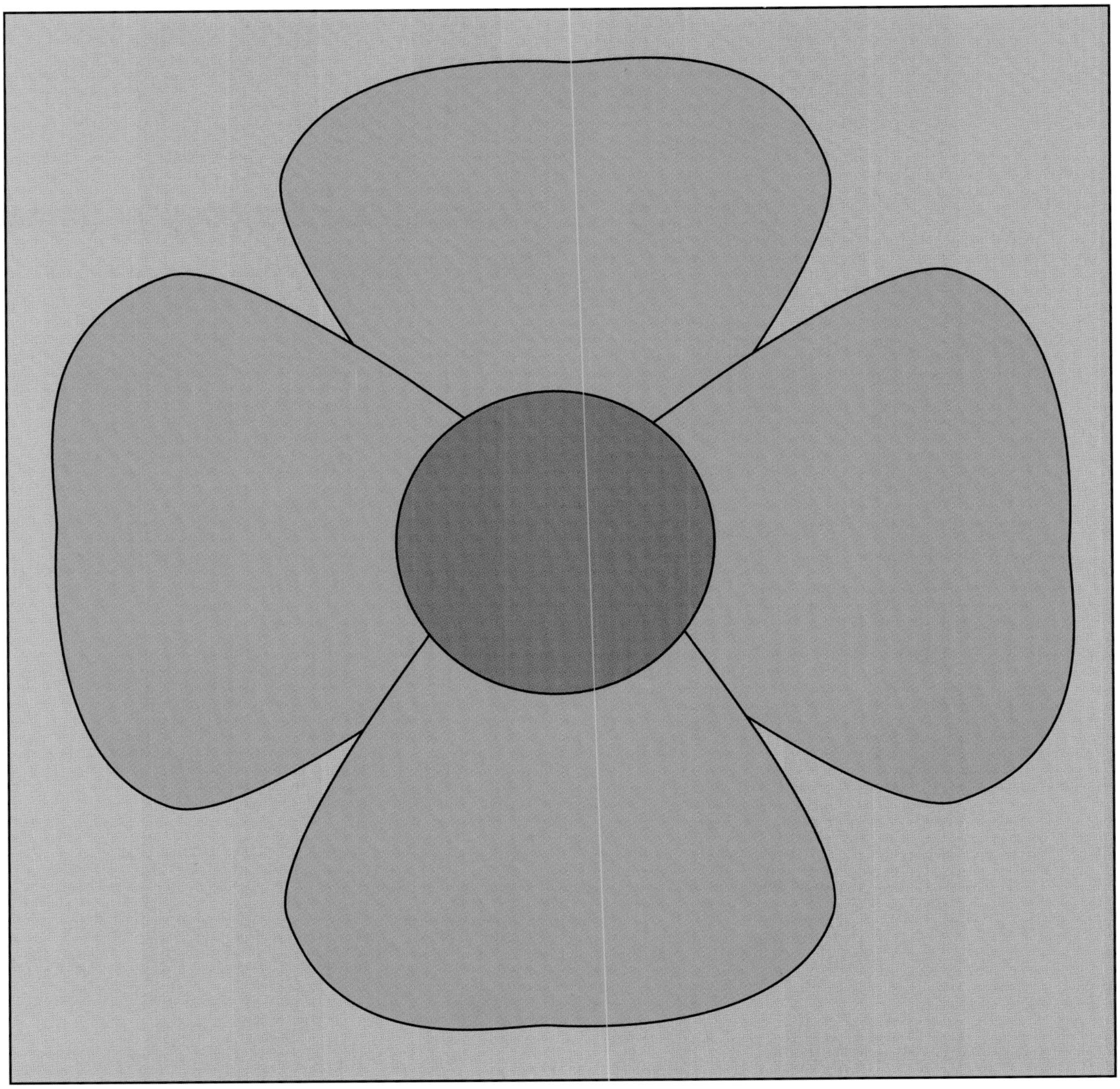

# 35. Pinwheel Blocks

April 20

Dear Friends,

Greetings from Pennsylvania. The sun is shining and the flowers are blooming. Roy has been getting the fields ready for planting corn. Our radish and lettuce plants are already up. We have had a good deal of rain to water the crops, so we have had a good start.

This Saturday we went to a sale of the late Marvin Fisher. Roy was able to buy some of his old farm equipment. They had a really good turnout at the sale and everything was gone within a few hours.

I bought some old Pinwheel blocks that his wife had done before she passed away. I finished hand piecing them together and have put the quilt top into the frame. I'm looking forward to quilting it with an all-over fan pattern.

On the way home, we stopped near the woods to look for some mushrooms. It is a really good time of the year here and mushrooms are very plentiful. We managed to fill two buckets and then headed home for supper. I canned some of the mushrooms and brought them over to our neighbor's for helping us build a fence for the chickens.

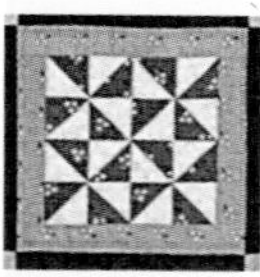

# 36. Windmill

April 30

Dear Friends,

I have been keeping busy trying to chase little Nora around the house. She is just starting to walk, and between her and Barbara, they keep me really going. Marlin and Vernon like being outside and are good at collecting eggs. I think they have named all the chickens in the pen.

Last Saturday we had a frolic here to put up a new windmill. We had a really windy storm here about two weeks ago and the windmill was torn down. The children really enjoyed watching the men put up the windmill. Most of the women helped prepare a large supper because the men were mighty hungry when they were finished. Our new windmill really pumps a lot of water, which we're very thankful for.

I finished my Roman Stripes quilt, except for the binding. I have the pieces cut out for another simple Four-Patch quilt. I'm just going to use scraps from other projects and not really worry about the colors.

*Martha*

# 37. Crops and Flowers

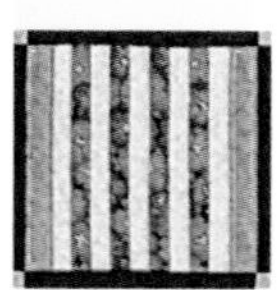

May 9

Dear Friends,

We have been working in the fields. The crops and the flowers are coming along very nicely. We enjoy living back in our district and the children really like your old home, Frieda. The children are enjoying the new chickens, as we did not have them on our old farm. Lyle's family has been over and is helping him get the farm up and running.

I spent yesterday with Henry at school. All of the children made a special drawing for their teacher depicting something they like about their school day. We put them in a special book with a letter from each of them and then presented it to her. At recess time, we had a nice picnic for the children. We also had them knot a comforter that we had especially put together for their teacher. This will be her last year teaching because she will be getting married in two weeks.

*Rebecca*

May 17

Dear Friends,

It seems like the days are getting warmer and there is much more work to be done outside. We spent the last two weeks planting and watering our vegetable garden. Raymond is going to let me keep the hired girl throughout the summer. She has become such a big help with getting the chores done. She is excited to be staying here this summer. She does go home on Saturday mornings to spend the weekend with her family.

Now that the children are home from school, our household is always busy. Raymond has been teaching Daniel and Noah more about working in the buggy and harness shop. The boys really seem to enjoy working with Raymond. Edith and Irene spend some time with me canning vegetables for the stand. The girls and I went mushrooming this past week and canned 56 quarts of mushrooms. Since they seem to be hard to find here, they were all sold within three days.

We're all going to the frolic tomorrow to build a new schoolhouse for our district. Last week there was a fire at the old schoolhouse and it burned down to the ground. We were very thankful that school was out for the summer. Tonight I have some chicken to prepare and pies to bake for the supper following the frolic.

Lavina

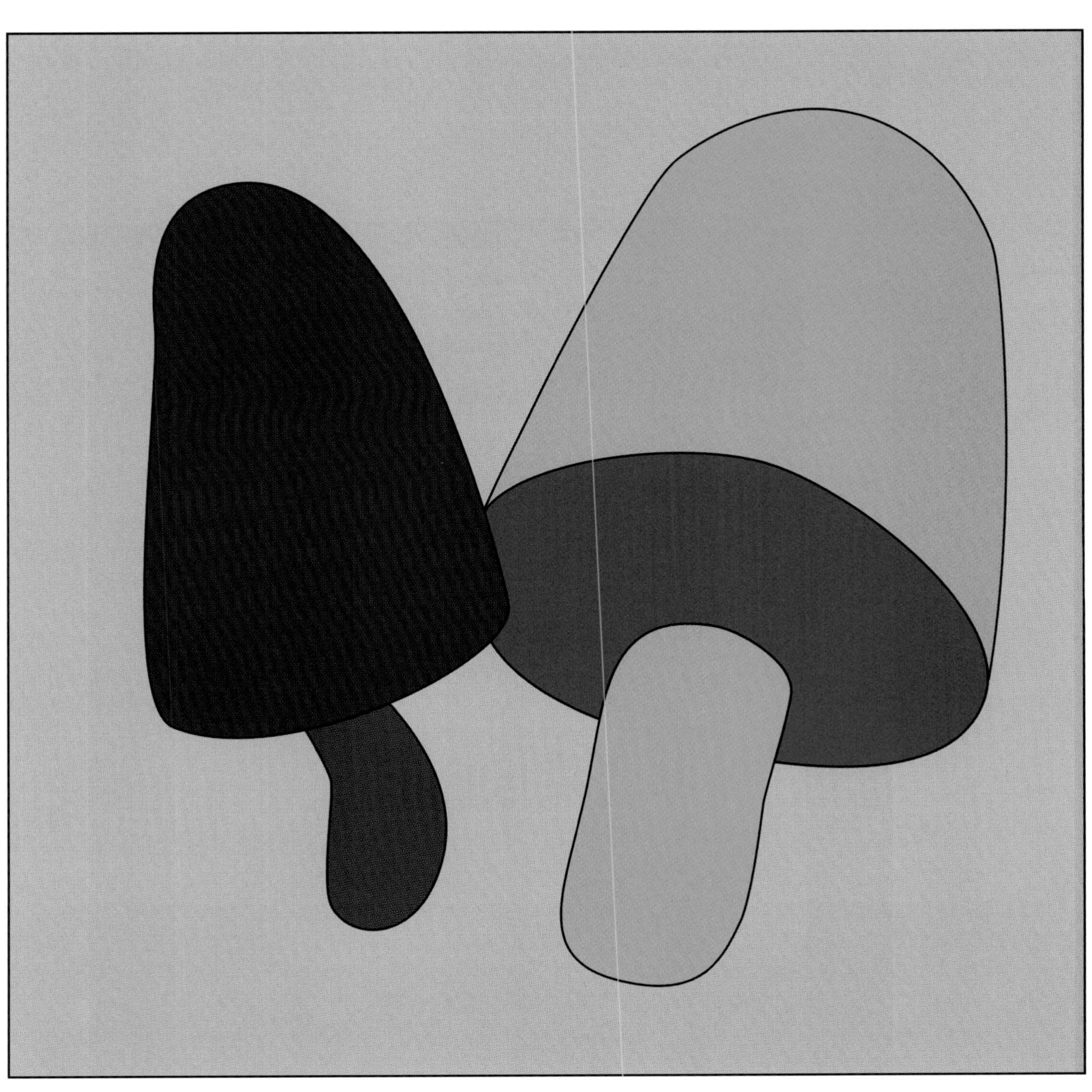

# 39. Shunning

May 28

Dear Friends,

I enjoyed reading all of your letters and catching up on what you are doing. Leroy bought 32 more dairy cows last week at the auction. Elvin and Melvin have been getting up earlier with Leroy, at about 5:00, to make sure they are all milked before breakfast. Naomi follows Ruth most of the day. Ruth enjoys sitting across from me at the quilt frame. I have begun to teach her how to hand piece squares together. Of course, little Naomi is right beside her.

There has not been a shunning in our district for quite awhile until this past Sunday. Daniel Weber's two sons who had joined the church last summer have decided that they cannot live by the church rules. They bought new cars and have begun to get in trouble with the law. It must be hard for their family to not be able to socialize with them. Proverbs 3:5,6.

# 40. Fireflies

June 5

Dear Friends,

It is hard to believe that Marvin and the children have been so easy to adjust to. Things are going very well here and I still smile every time one of those darling children calls me Mama. Marvin's farm is very large. It used to be the family farm and now he and three of his brothers and their families live on the property. I have enjoyed getting to know his brother's families. All four of us women are quilters. We have been working on some quilts together and it sure is a big help when you need someone to help you put one on the frame. Just today they were all here and helped me put a crazy quilt in my frame. The crazy patches are set on a point and are made using wool scraps.

Yesterday we had such a nice family gathering by the lake. All four families packed supper and headed off to eat and play softball. Altogether there are 24 of us. We sang some of our favorite hymns and started to get ready to head home because it was getting dark. Timothy and Joseph took a few empty jars and filled them with fireflies to light our path. They gave Edith her own jar of fireflies. When we arrived home she cried, as she had to let them go.

*Frieda*

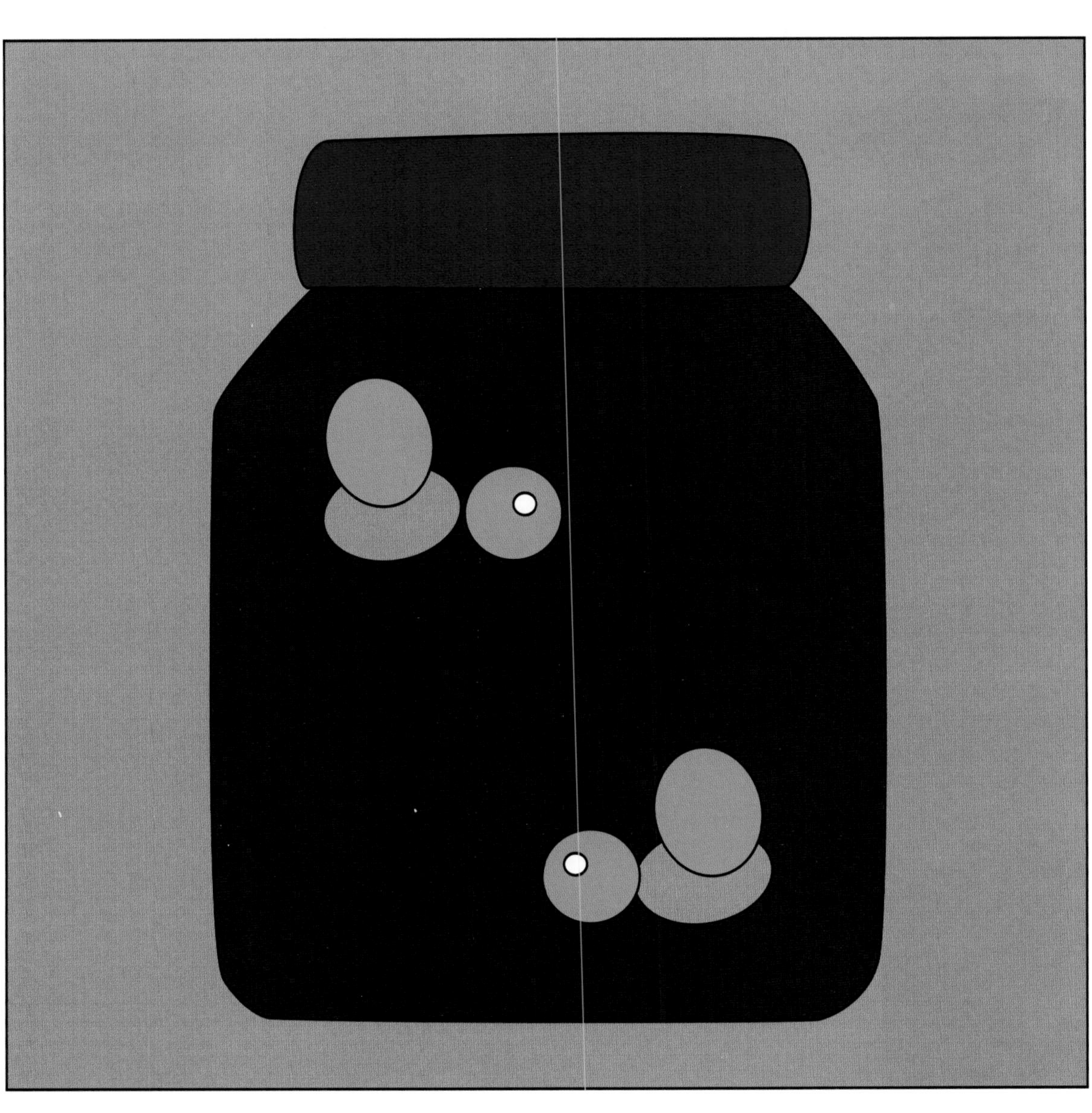

# 41. Ocean Waves

June 16

Dear Friends,

Dan and the children all seem to be doing well. Karen and Emery will be one year-olds next month and are just beginning to walk. It seems like when I am working in the kitchen, one of them is now hanging on to my apron. The fields are planted and the gardens are blooming. We had a really good batch of strawberries and raspberries this season. I have canned over 50 quarts of each. I am taking some tomorrow to the bake sale that is being held to help our neighbor, John Miller, with some hospital bills.

I have finally finished my Ocean Waves quilt. It seems like that one was in the frame longer than most. My three sisters came over last week and helped me with the binding. They also helped me get my Hole in the Barn Door quilt on the frame. Our reunion is only a couple of months away and I know that Rachel is getting her quilt top ready for us to work on.

# 42. Strawberries and Raspberries

June 21

Dear Friends,

We have spent the last week picking our raspberries and strawberries. Mary and Faye were in charge of that chore. The boys tried to help, but seemed more interested in eating them. We had fresh strawberry pie for supper tonight.

Abe really enjoyed the addition that most of you helped him build. He hasn't had as much time lately to spend in the furniture shop because he is so busy in the fields. The tourists continually stop here, so I have been spending more of my time helping out in the shop. Word travels fast and he has quite a few orders already for things he will be working on this winter.

I have been working on a Friendship quilt. I have enclosed a piece of muslin for all of you to sign and then embroider your names on. You can either put it in the envelope with your circle letter or bring it with you to the reunion. Mary and Faye are also making a block. See you all at the reunion.

*Ida*

# 43. Eight-Pointed Star

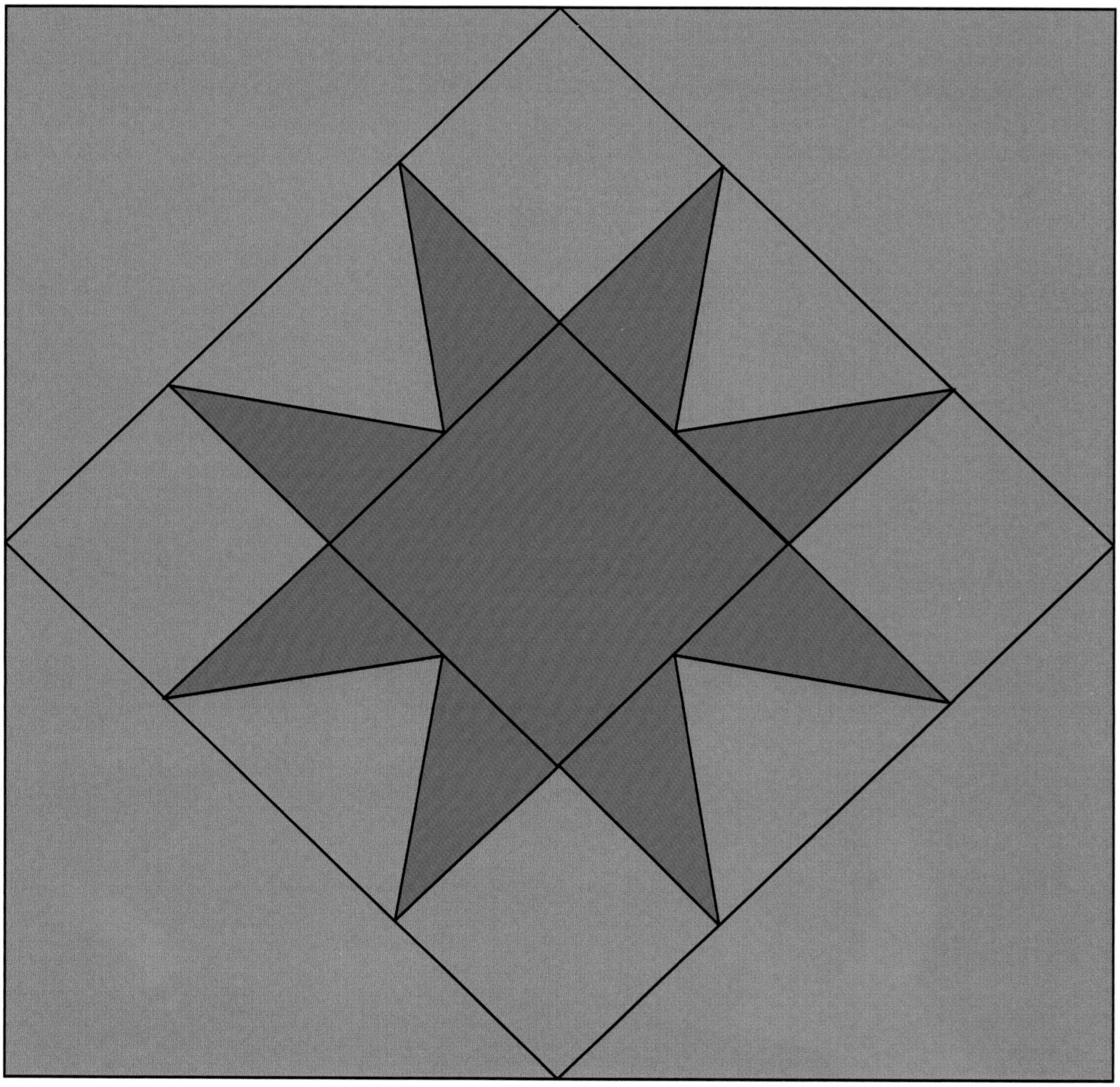

June 30

Dear Friends,

Greetings from Ohio. The weather here has been quite hot in the 90s. We could really use some rain for the crops. We spent last weekend in Pennsylvania at our family reunion. Freeman was glad to see his family. There were over 200 of us attending. He has talked a few of his brother's older sons into coming to work on the farm. We seem to be having a bad case of alfalfa weevils. Freeman is having a hard time getting rid of them and they seem to be destroying some of the crop. Between the weevils and no rain, our crop yield will not be very high.

The children are well. Martha is already 10, but it doesn't seem possible. Nathan spends a lot of time helping Freeman with the livestock. Ivan and David are almost inseparable. Lydiann is talking as much as Katie.

There has not been much time to quilt the past few months; I have been hand piecing a Spider Web Star quilt using various scraps. My Eight-Pointed Star quilt is half finished.

*Regina*

# 44. Family Fish Fry

July 12

Dear Friends,

I am enjoying my new family. Daniel keeps very busy being the bishop of this district. Dale is learning so much about farm life from Jacob and Andy. We both are so happy in our new home.

Most of Daniel's family still lives in this district. Last night we had so much fun going down to the lake for a family fish fry. The men and boys enjoyed fishing together. Daniel has taught Dale the fundamentals of fishing. It was an exciting evening and Dale managed to catch two 12-pound bass. It seems as if we have always been a part of this family.

Some of the women in the family are quilters and some are embroiderers. I am very interested in learning how to embroider tea towels. Daniel's sister gave me one of her tea towels and some basic lessons. In return, I am giving them some basic lessons on how to hand piece Monkey Wrench blocks together. It was soon time to fry the fish and get supper ready. We ended with a singing and sang all the way home.

Miriam

# 45. Rail Fence

July 21

Dear Friends,

Good news! God was with us through the last couple of trying months. We are so thankful that Samuel has been able to resume his work on the farm. He is feeling stronger every day. We are very much looking forward to having the reunion here next month. Regina's family will be staying at our home and Lydiann's family will be staying at Martha's.

I have a Rail Fence quilt made with purple and blue fabrics that I will have for us to quilt. I was hoping to have my Basket quilt ready, but I still have four more blocks to hand piece. It will be fun for all of us to be together again. I am so glad that all of you continue to send your quilt patterns with the circle letter.

*Rachel*

# 46. Blueberry Ice Cream

August 12

Dear Friends,

We have just returned to Pennsylvania and really enjoyed our visit and the reunion. The children had so much fun and especially enjoyed making the blueberry and raspberry ice cream. We are going to be making some blueberry ice cream tonight. I will enjoy watching Katie pick out each blueberry and eat it before she eats her ice cream.

We enjoyed working on your Rail Fence quilt, Rachel. I am glad that we were able to finish it and even had time to put on the binding. It was so nice to see all of your latest quilting projects. The Pinwheel quilt that I am working on is almost finished. I was thinking that since I purchased these Pinwheel blocks of Martha Fisher's, I would like to present it to one of her granddaughters. I thought it would make a nice remembrance of her grandmother.

Lydiann

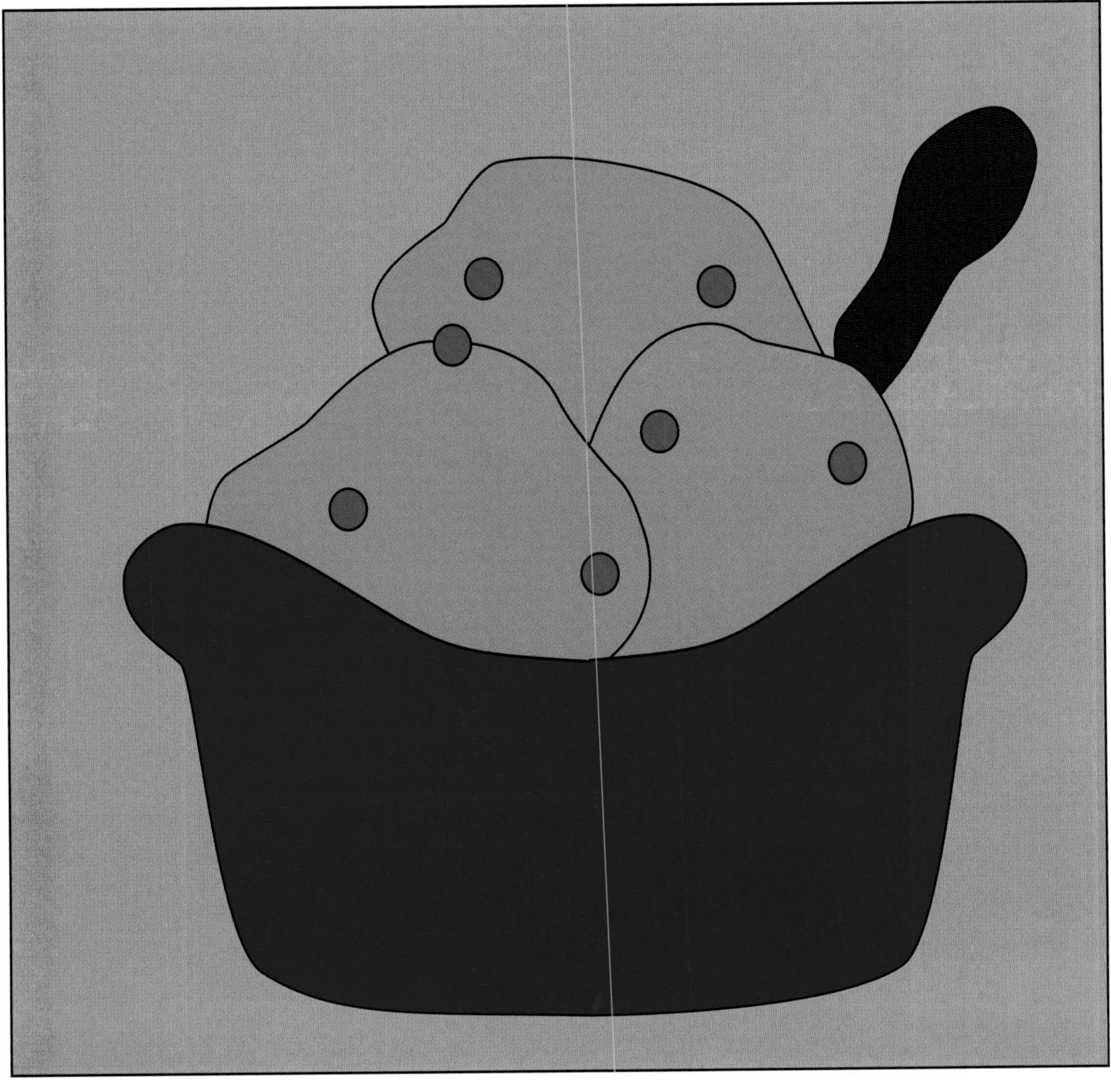

# 47. Four-Patch

August 19

Dear Friends,

It is a nice sunny day with a cool breeze. We have been very busy taking care of the corn in the fields. The workhorses have been really getting a good workout this week. Our corn production is going to be higher this year. Eli has had to hire a few of our neighbor's sons to help him out. He was out milking the cows on Tuesday and was kicked by Bessie. He broke his wrist and that has slowed him down a bit.

The children are doing well and are still talking about our quilt reunion. Today I am sending a Four-Patch pattern with my circle letter. I have most of my blocks pieced together for my Four-Patch quilt. It will be nice to be working on it this fall. Next week some of the women from our school district are going to get together with some of the women from Ida's school district. We're going to work on a couple of quilts for the Joseph Miller family. They lost most of their home to a fire. The family is also going to be scheduling a few work frolics to help rebuild their home.

I have been spending a lot of time in the kitchen baking and canning. Marlin is very excited about starting school next week. Vernon just doesn't understand why he is not old enough to go with him. I will close for now, as it is time to get back to my chores.

*Martha*

# 48. Vegetable Garden

August 24

Dear Friends,

Henry and Andy started school today along with the other children in our district. It seems a lot quieter this morning without them. Lyle and his brother have spent most of the week threshing the wheat and taking care of the fields. Our vegetable garden supplied us with squash, corn, carrots, beets, cucumbers and beans this year. I am very thankful that our basement is stocked for the winter. I'm going over this afternoon to help my sister-in-law with her canning. I have a good supply of fresh corn and squash to take her.

I have been working on the little blocks that we have been sending each other in this circle letter. Do you realize that we have over 40 blocks already? I didn't realize it until I pulled out all my blocks and laid them out. I also am working on the Sunshine and Shadow in the Square quilt top that I brought to the reunion. I put it in the frame today. I have drawn out a grapevine border for the outer border. I am going to use a feathered vine in the large triangles with a feathered wreath in the center.

Rebecca

# 49. Flying Geese

September 6

Dear Friends,

Our home is much quieter during the day with our five oldest children in school. We are finishing up with our apple season, so Raymond will be spending more time in his shop. We let our hired girl return to her home. I have missed her company. She finished quilting my Nine-Patch quilt before she left. I decided to let her take it with her because she was such a big help this summer. I am working on piecing together blocks using the Jacob's Ladder pattern.

Last week Martha's family was blessed with a new addition to the family. Aden is the name they have chosen for their new son. He looks so much like his brothers. I took over a Flying Geese quilt that I had made for him.

We had a paint frolic at one of our elderly neighbor's home. There were 16 of us women and we managed to give the inside of the home a fresh coat of paint. We had a really nice lunch that his wife, Lonnia Bollinger, provided for us. We even had an hour to sit down with her at her quilt frame. She is such a good storyteller that time went by so fast. She told us so many stories of when she was a little girl. I am going to share some of them with my children tonight.

Lavina

# 50. Missing Cows

September 12

Dear Friends,

We started out with a very exciting morning. Leroy and the boys went out to the barn to milk the cows. The cows were nowhere in sight. They discovered that the gate to the fence was open. They took the buggy, along with a few of the neighbors, and set out to search for them. They found them about a mile down the road in one of our neighbor's front yards. The neighbor was not upset, but had to laugh saying that the grass probably won't need a cutting this week. Two hours later, the cows had been milked and were back in our pasture.

I have enjoyed working on the Bar quilt that I have in the frame so much. Ruth enjoys keeping my needles threaded. Naomi really likes watching us. I think my girls are going to be quilters just like my mom and grandmother. I have not been taking in as many quilts from my English customers. I'm going to start making some of my quilts for my children so that I can present them as gifts upon their marriage.

Edna

# 51. Crazy Quilt

September 21

Dear Friends,

I had a sisters quilting day here yesterday. There were seven of us present. Marvin's three sisters and my three sisters all came with their children. I think the children had as much fun as we did. A few of the older girls helped prepare lunch and took care of the younger children. We managed to finish my crazy quilt. The binding is on. It seems much heavier with all the wool scraps that I used.

The children are doing well. Timothy and Joseph really enjoy school. Little Edith spends the day with me picking vegetables or helping me in the kitchen. We love to sing hymns together as we do our chores.

Marvin and his brothers went to a land auction to see if they could get any used farm equipment. They returned with some new shovels, rakes and small garden tools. They also bought a new plow for the horses. We all had a family dinner together. We had fresh peach cobbler, apple pies and carrot bread topped with homemade ice cream.

*Frieda*

## 52. Pennsylvania Dutch Heritage

October 8

Dear Friends,

I am enjoying the cooler days of fall. Most of the garden has been cleared for next year. Most of the flowers are dead early this year because we have had a few cold nights with low temperatures and frost.

Dan's father passed away last month. They had a sale of his possessions that was open just for family members. Next week they will have a sale for the public for what was left over. Dan purchased a few things for the farm. He also purchased an old hutch that his mother had in the kitchen. It has been in their family for many years. It is an unusual piece of furniture. It has a distinctive design on the doors. The design represents our Pennsylvania Dutch heritage. I traced part of that design and have included that with my circle letter as my block.

The children and I spent the day in the kitchen. We baked some bread and canned beans. Then we made some homemade doughnuts. Dan knew what we were up to the minute he walked in the house. He could smell the fresh doughnuts. Of course, he could also see the smiles that all five of his children had on their faces. Making doughnuts is one of their favorite things to do.

*Lavern*

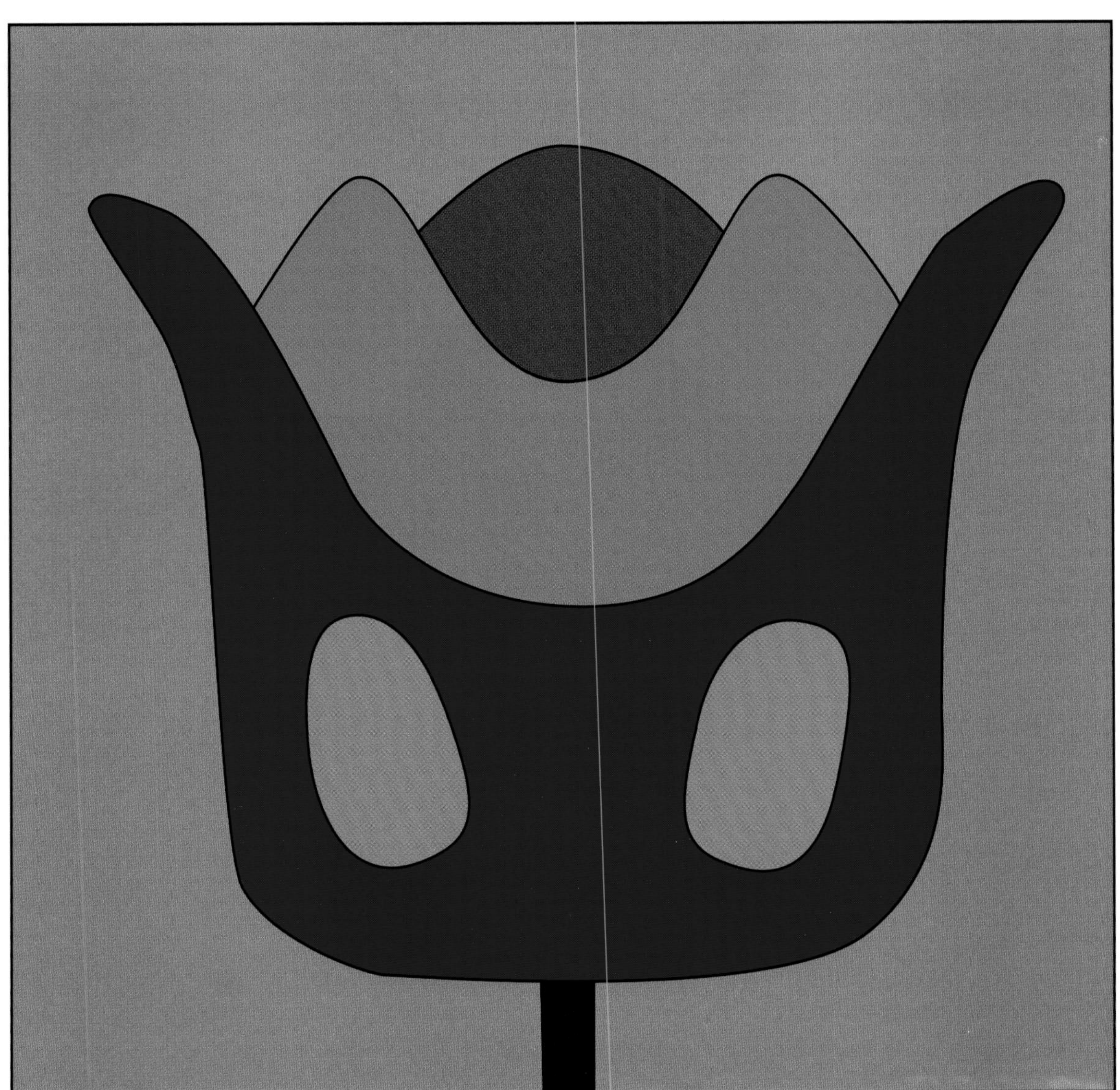

# 53. Signature Squares

October 19

Dear Friends,

It is a nice, cool, fall day. The sun is shining and the temperature is 60 degrees. I really had a scare this morning as I was driving the buggy to town. There was a car full of English tourists who kept trying to take a photograph of the children and me in the buggy. They were driving too close and not paying attention to the road and I had to swerve around another car. The horse was spooked, but I was able to get her under control. The English did not give up and followed us to the grocer's. They still continued to take our photographs. I was glad that our trip home was uneventful.

Thank you all for sending the squares that you signed for me. I have been putting them together with the pattern I have enclosed. I'm hand piecing them together. I have also collected some friendship squares from other quilters in our area.

The children are doing well. Mary and Faye are both getting ready to cut out their next quilt. Both grandmothers are coming over tomorrow to help them cut out the pieces and plan what to do next. Nettie is starting to get very active and crawling all around. The boys spent the day helping Abe with some simple chores in the furniture shop. I will close for now, as it is time to get dinner started.

*Ida*

# 54. Deacon

November 1

Dear Friends,

Sunday was an important day for our family. We spent the week getting ready to have church services at our home. The benches arrived on Saturday and were placed in our living room and kitchen. We prepared a light lunch for after the service and all seemed ready.

Freeman and three other members of our church were in the lot to become a deacon. The four Bibles were placed on the table. When Freeman's Bible was opened, there was the paper with a verse on it inside. So we knew that the lot had fallen on him to be the new deacon.

About 90 attended the service. We served lunch and some continued to visit after lunch. At nighttime, some of the benches were taken to the barn. The youth returned for their singing. It was nice to sit on the porch and hear them singing some of our favorite hymns.

*Regina*

# 55. Checkers

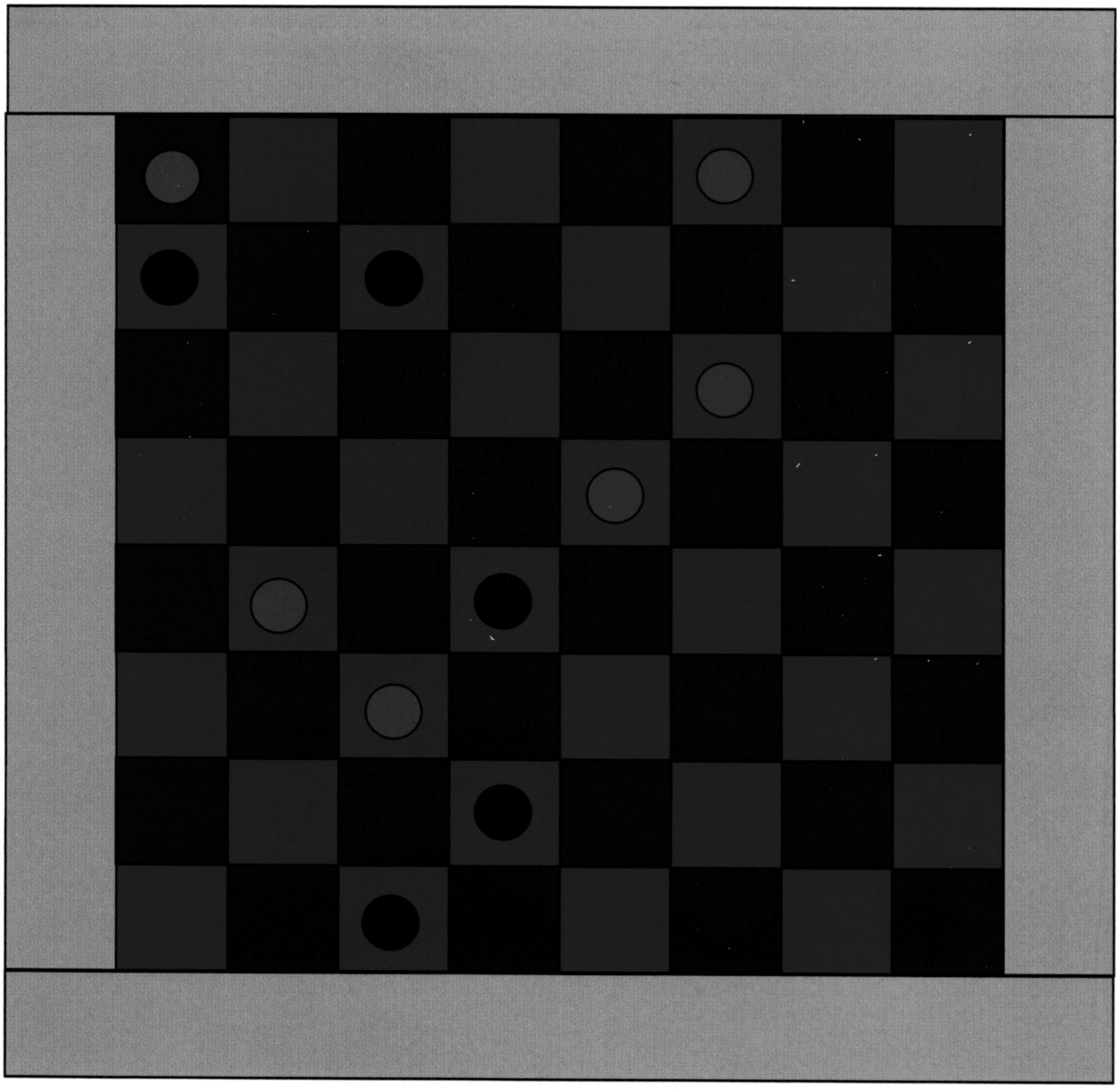

November 14

Dear Friends,

The weather here is becoming much cooler. It is early morning and breakfast is finished. Daniel gave the boys their chores for the day at breakfast. He will be gone today to preside at a wedding. Yesterday he presided as bishop for the funeral for Benjamin King. When he is gone working as bishop for our district, the boys do as many farm chores as possible.

Last Saturday we had Daniel's family over to our home for supper. After dinner, the boys spent some time playing checkers in the kitchen. The girls decided to make some dolls out of cornhusks. Then Daniel hitched up the horses to the wagon and we all went for a hayride.

My Monkey Wrench quilt is almost all together. I have one more row of blocks to attach. I have enjoyed learning more about embroidery. I have even given Katie a hoop and she sits with me and practices her stitches.

# 56. Gasoline Lamp

November 20

Dear Friends,

We woke up this morning with frost covering the ground. The days are becoming cooler. It was time to put the straw hats away and bring out the felt hats for the boys. We also brought out some of the other winter clothing. Samuel explained what chores had to be done today to us at breakfast. He is going to a frolic to help rebuild Mahlon Oberholtzer's buggy shop that burned down last month.

I took the girls with me to the fabric store today. One of our English neighbors drove us to town since Samuel had taken the buggy to the frolic. We bought some bleached muslin for quilt backing. I have finished a Grandmother's Choice quilt top. I pieced the blocks on my treadle sewing machine. I used muslin for the background and the patchwork was a solid purple. Lena and Martha helped me get my quilt sandwiched this evening so tomorrow we will work on putting it in the frame. The days seem to be getting dark so early. I'm sitting near the gasoline lamp as I'm writing my letter. The house is quiet and everyone has gone to bed.

*Rachel*

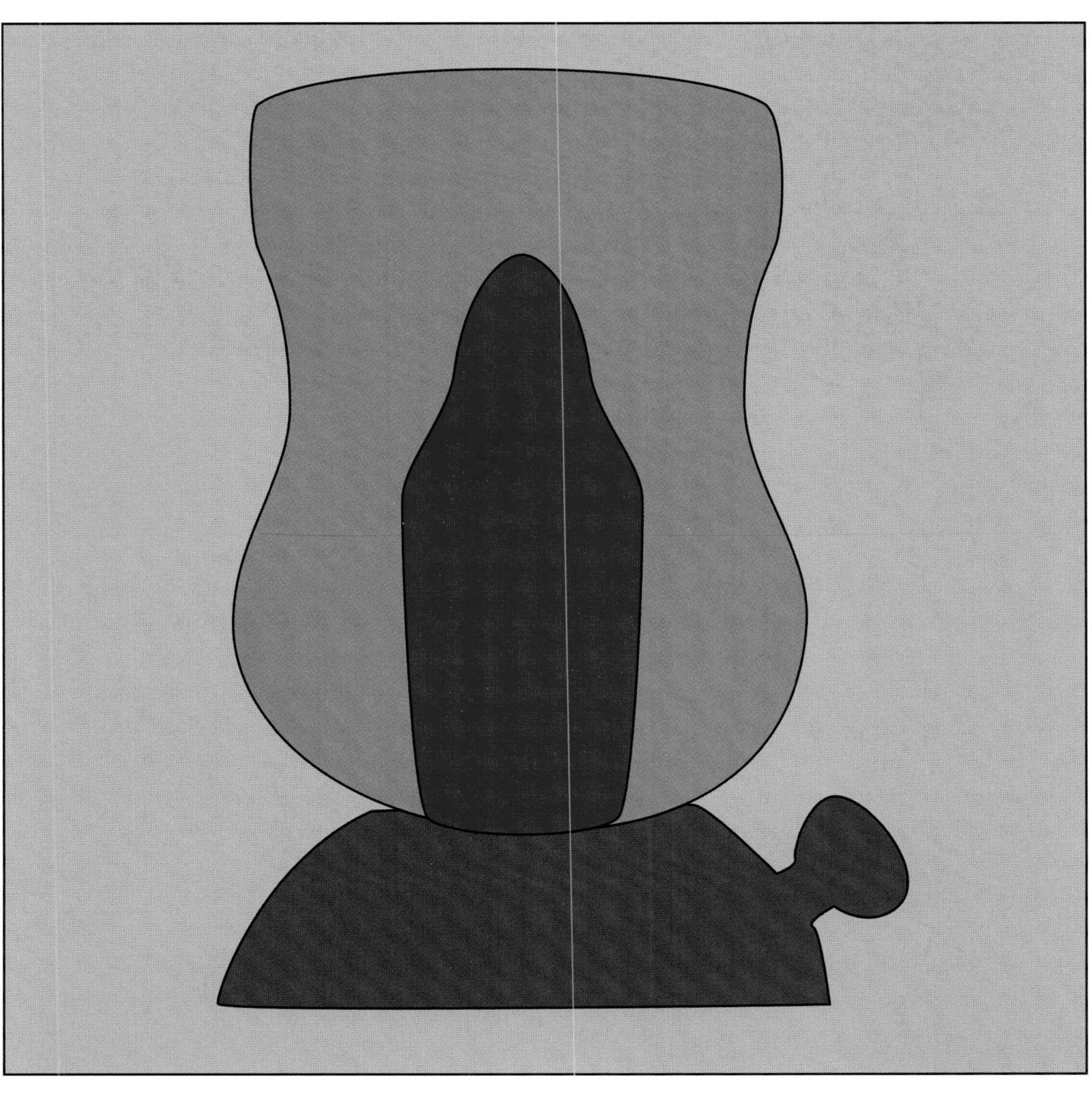

# 57. Streak of Lightning

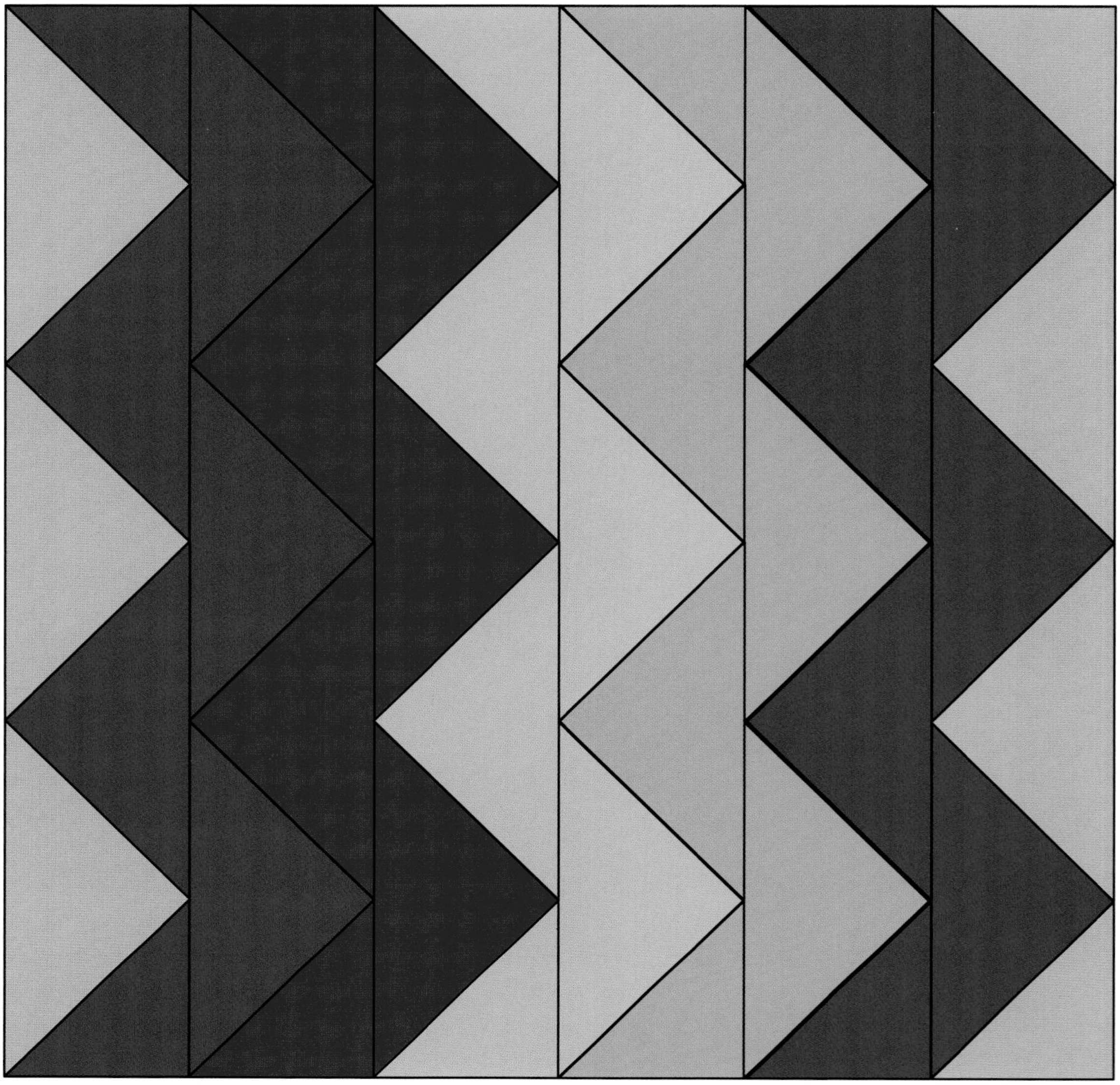

December 3

Dear Friends,

The weather down here in Pennsylvania is getting much cooler also. Roy has been busy taking care of the livestock and working more in his blacksmith shop now that the fieldwork is done. His family gathered here this past weekend to celebrate his parents' 35th wedding anniversary. We presented them with 35 gifts. They were surprised, as they thought we were just getting together for a quilting. It was such a nice day and full of so much enjoyment as we reminisced and shared stories. The children especially enjoyed the stories that their grandfather told.

We even had enough time to put my Streak of Lightning quilt in the frame. I have enclosed a pattern of my quilt as my block. I used various colors, using scraps from some old shirts and dresses that were no longer recyclable. They were given to me from some old clothes that Roy's mother had in her attic.

On Tuesday I will be going to Roy's mother's home for a quilting. We are going to be working on a quilt for her youngest daughter that was published to be married last week. We're going to make a plain quilt with a center medallion of a feathered wreath. We will also be doing some crosshatching in the background. Roy's mother has a large quilt frame that drops from her ceiling. We can fit quite a few women all around her frame as the top will be fully stretched out when we began. She has invited around 20 women to the quilting.

Lydiann

# 58. Christmas Cookies

December 17

Dear Friends,

Our family has adjusted very well to our new son, Aden, who was born in September. He is a very good baby and seems very content just to be watching all the activity that goes on in our kitchen. Eli's broken wrist has healed well.

Yesterday, we spent the day at Rachel's home. The children enjoyed making sugar cookies for Christmas out of various shapes. They liked rolling out the dough and some of the younger children smiled when we cut the shape out and placed it on the cookie sheet. We also made some oatmeal and molasses cookies. We had such a nice day just visiting with each other.

We will be going to my brother's district to visit him for Christmas and to their children's school to see their Christmas program. The next day we will gather at his home for Christmas dinner with most of my family. We are hoping that the weather cooperates because of it being a two-hour buggy ride.

*Martha*

# 59. Sunshine and Shadow

December 26

Dear Friends,

On Christmas Eve, we went to school to see Henry and Andy perform in a skit that their teacher had planned. We all really enjoyed the day and sang some Christmas carols before we left. On Christmas Day, we had a quiet dinner with just his brother and his family. We gave the boys new sleds for Christmas. Susie received some wooden toy animals. Lyle presented me with a new wooden sewing box and he received a new lunch pail.

Today we are going to have dinner at Lyle's brother's home. I have some canned goods and cookies ready to take. They also invited the Andrew Gingerich family to join us. They are staying on my brother's property, waiting for some land to become available. Most of their family lives in Wisconsin and the weather was too cold for them to make the trip home. They have been a big help to my brother with his farm this year.

My Sunshine and Shadow in the Square quilt is finished. The grapevine border fit the quilt very well. I have been hand piecing a Cross in the Square quilt. The blocks are almost done and are made with wool scraps. Well, I had better close for now and get ready for dinner.

*Rebecca*

# 60. Teapot

December 30

Dear Friends,

We had a very busy Christmas with a lot of company. Raymond gave me a new teapot for Christmas, which came in very handy with all the relatives that came to visit on Christmas and second Christmas. It was quiet when the children returned back to school on the 27th. I am glad that they don't take a Christmas break like the English children do. It is much nicer to have them out of school in April when there is so much to do on the farm.

The children are doing very well and this spring Raymond has plans to add on an addition to our home. He would like to add on a separate bedroom for the older boys because they're up so early helping with chores. The boys are really learning how to become farmers. They also are learning how to assemble and fix buggies.

I have been teaching Edith and Irene how to hand quilt. They have been helping me quilt my Jacob's Ladder quilt. They have no problem when it comes to straight lines. It is when they try to quilt circles or curves that it becomes more difficult for them. Little Roseanna threads the needle for them with a big smile on her face and keeps saying "practice practice."

Lavina

# 61. Bar Quilt

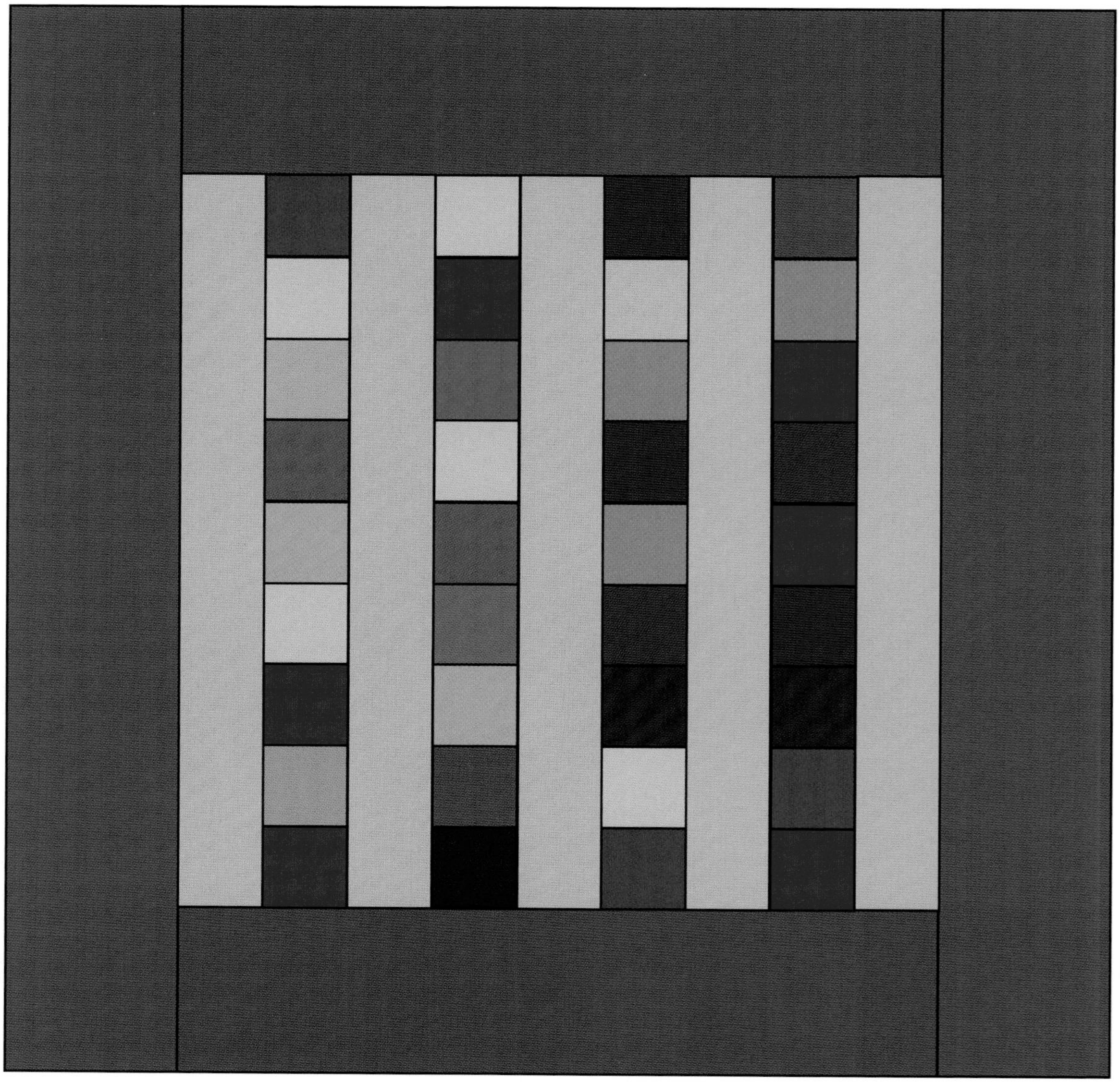

January 6

Dear Friends,

The weather here has been bitterly cold this past week. It was so cold and icy yesterday that we were unable to attend church. The temperature is well below zero with about three new feet of snow. The children have been riding to school with the neighbor in his sleigh all week.

I know I had mentioned to you before about the shunning in our district. Daniel Weber's sons have both returned to the church. They asked for God's forgiveness and were reinstated by a unanimous vote of the church congregation. They have both given up their new cars and have turned over the money to their father to help them invest in a farm.

The girls and I spent some of the night tonight working on my Bar quilt. Not only is Ruth keeping my needles threaded, but she is also starting to take a few stitches. I sat at the frame and told them some stories about how I used to sit at the frame with my sisters and help my mom. They just giggled and couldn't believe I was ever a little girl.

# 62. Cradle

January 16

Dear Friends,

Last week we were truly blessed with a daughter, who we named Wilma, after her great-grandmother. She is sleeping in a cradle that Ida's husband made and is covered with a quilt that Rachel and Martha brought over last week. She is a very good baby and the children are really enjoying her. Marvin's family has been so much help to us. They have been bringing over meals and helping me with the household chores. Proverbs 22:6.

Marvin's sisters were here today and we spent the afternoon making half-moon pies. We cooked the apples as the children rolled the pie dough and cut it into circles. Soon the apples were spread on the pie dough and put in the oven. We made over 100 half-moon pies. There were enough pies for a snack and some to take home for our families for dessert.

My quilt frame has a Bar quilt on it. It has nine patches in every other bar. I am hand piecing some of the extra nine patches to make a baby quilt. My quilts seem to be getting finished faster because when Marvin's sisters come to visit, they like to visit and talk around the quilt frame.

*Frieda*

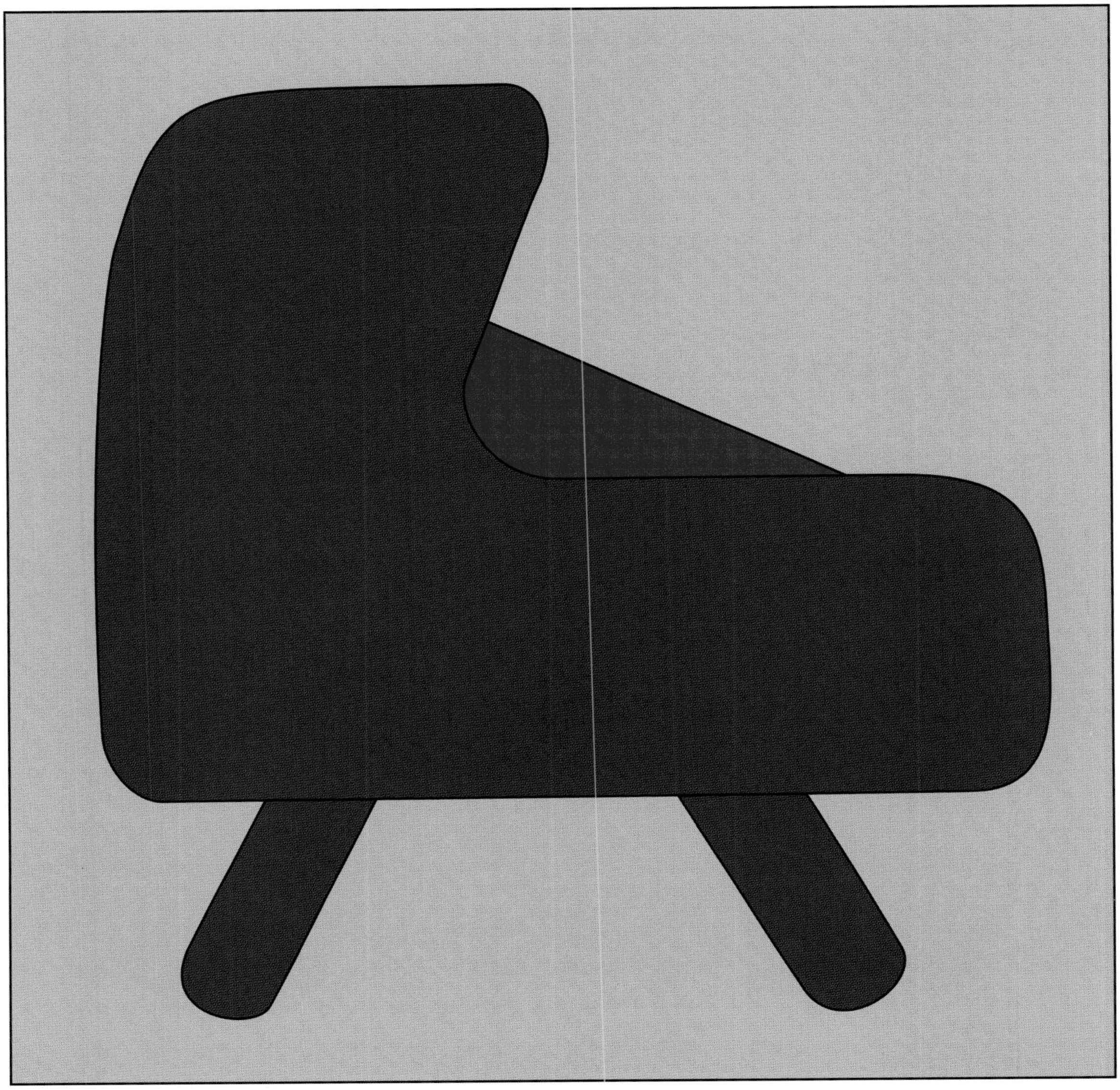

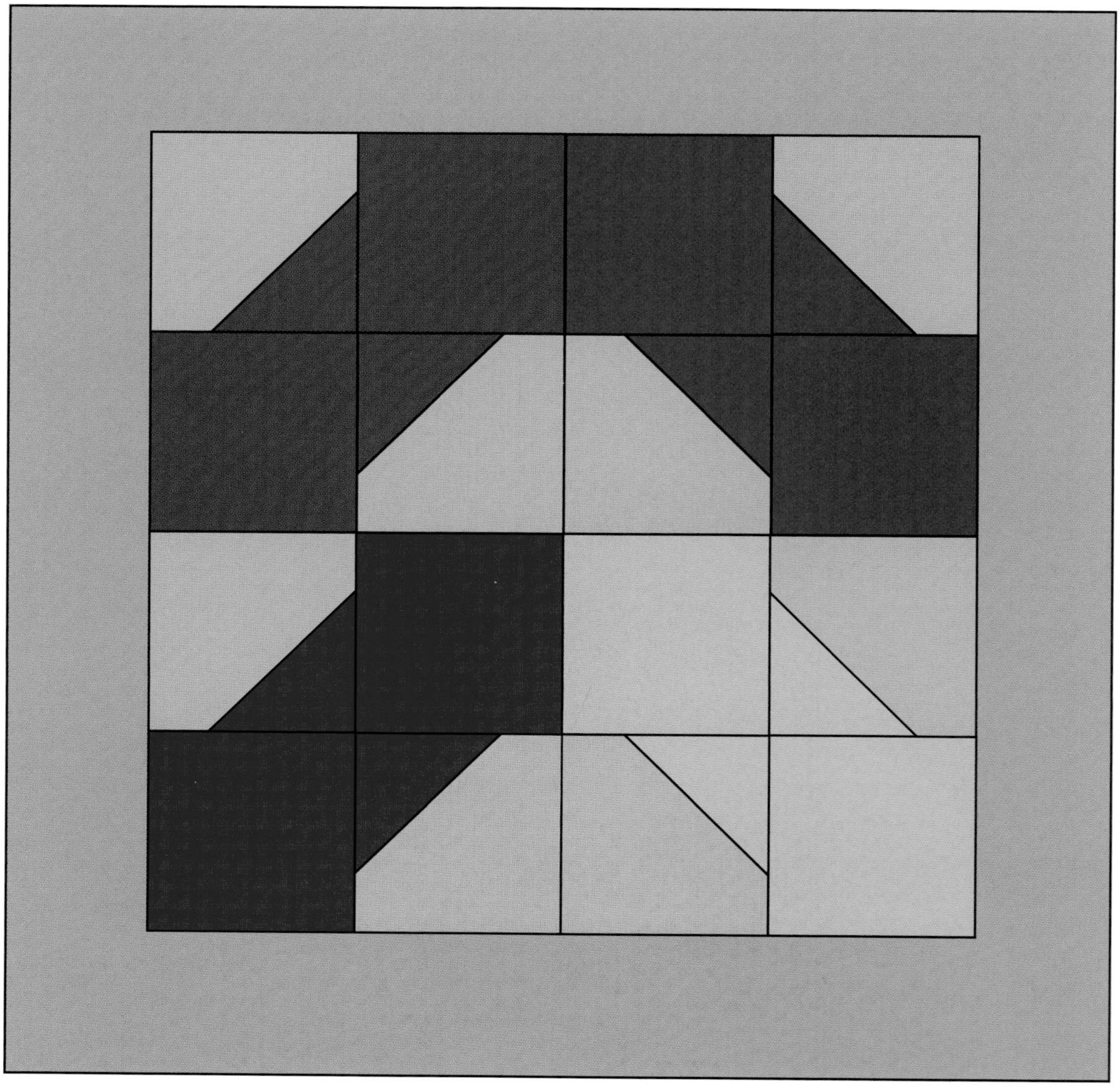

# 63. Bow Tie

January 30

Dear Friends,

Our family is looking forward to the warmer weather. We went to visit Frieda's family this afternoon. Her family is doing very well. We took them some chicken soup and apple pie. It seemed like the afternoon went so fast. We ended up staying for supper. After supper, we took out her little box of all the patterns we have been trading. She has been doing all her blocks with wool scraps. She is using a black embroidery stitch around all of her appliqué blocks.

Today I have enclosed the pattern for a Bow Tie quilt. It is the pattern that I have been piecing on my treadle sewing machine. I have been using some scraps from leftover clothing. They have been in my ragbag for quite awhile. I have enough pieces cut out for my quilt top. Next week I'm going to take what is left of the rags and sew them together to make a new rag rug for my kitchen.

# 64. Wood Stove

February 10

Dear Friends,

Yesterday I spent some of the day visiting the children at school. I took some chicken soup with me, which I kept warm on the wood stove. The students enjoyed the warm soup with their lunch. There was no recess today, as the weather was too cold. It was good to hear some of the children read from the German Bible. The older children are also able to recite the Lord's prayer in German. Some of the older children also help tutor the younger children. Their teacher, Ada Yoder, has been teaching there for six years now.

We're hoping for warmer weather next week. The snow is over four feet in some places. Eugene has been keeping busy filling our wood box. Abe took two cords of wood to the neighbor's yesterday, as their supply was running low. This seems to be one of the coldest winters on record.

Simon and John spent most of their day in the house with Nettie and me. Mary and Faye helped me put the binding on my Friendship quilt. Mary is working on a Flying Geese quilt while Faye is working on a Log Cabin quilt. I have just put an Irish Chain quilt in my frame. One day last week, I went to a quilting at Elnora Bontrager's home. Mary and Faye were asked to sit at the quilt frame instead of watching the children. They thought it was very nice to be asked to quilt.

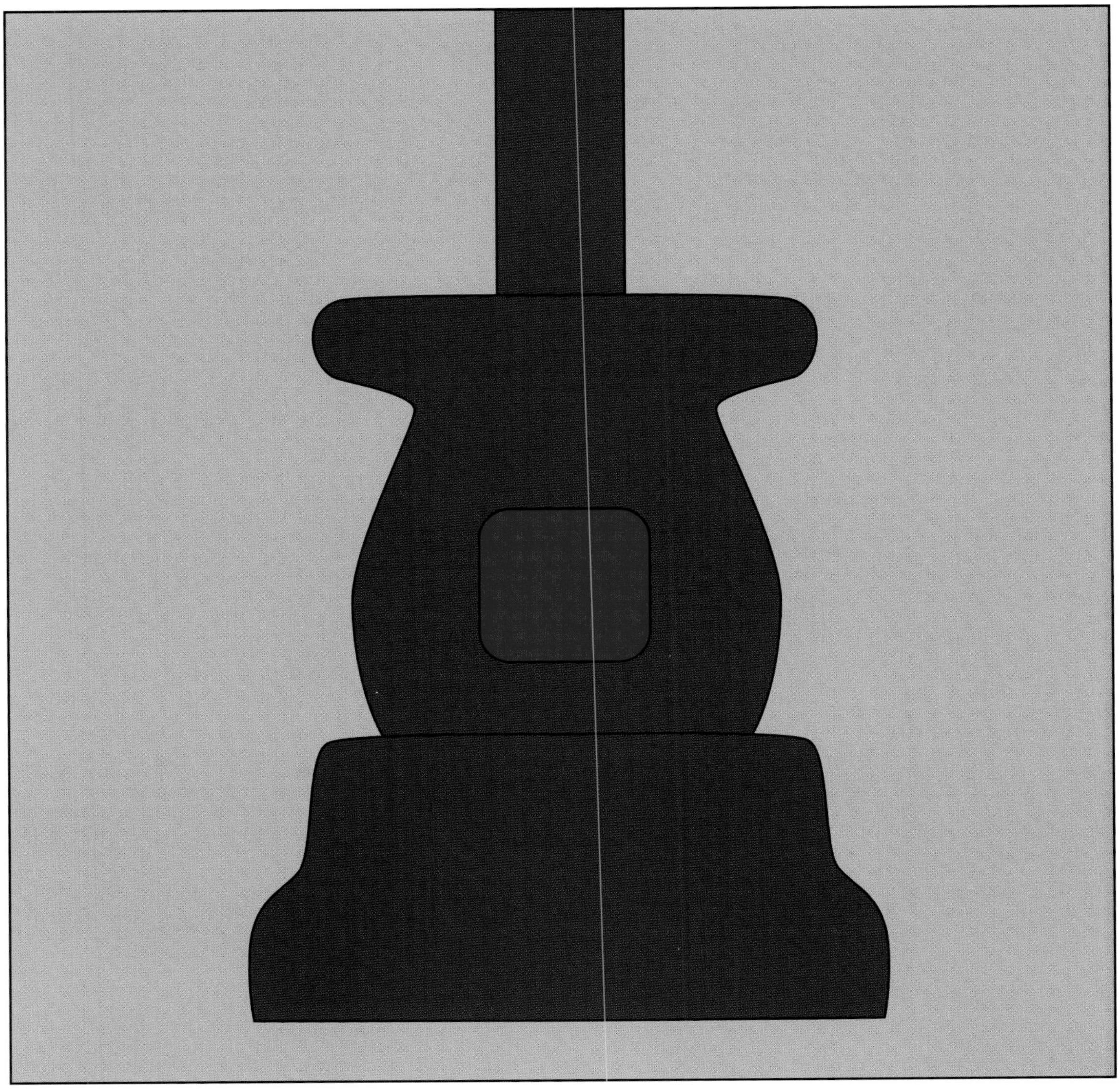

# 65. Hexagons

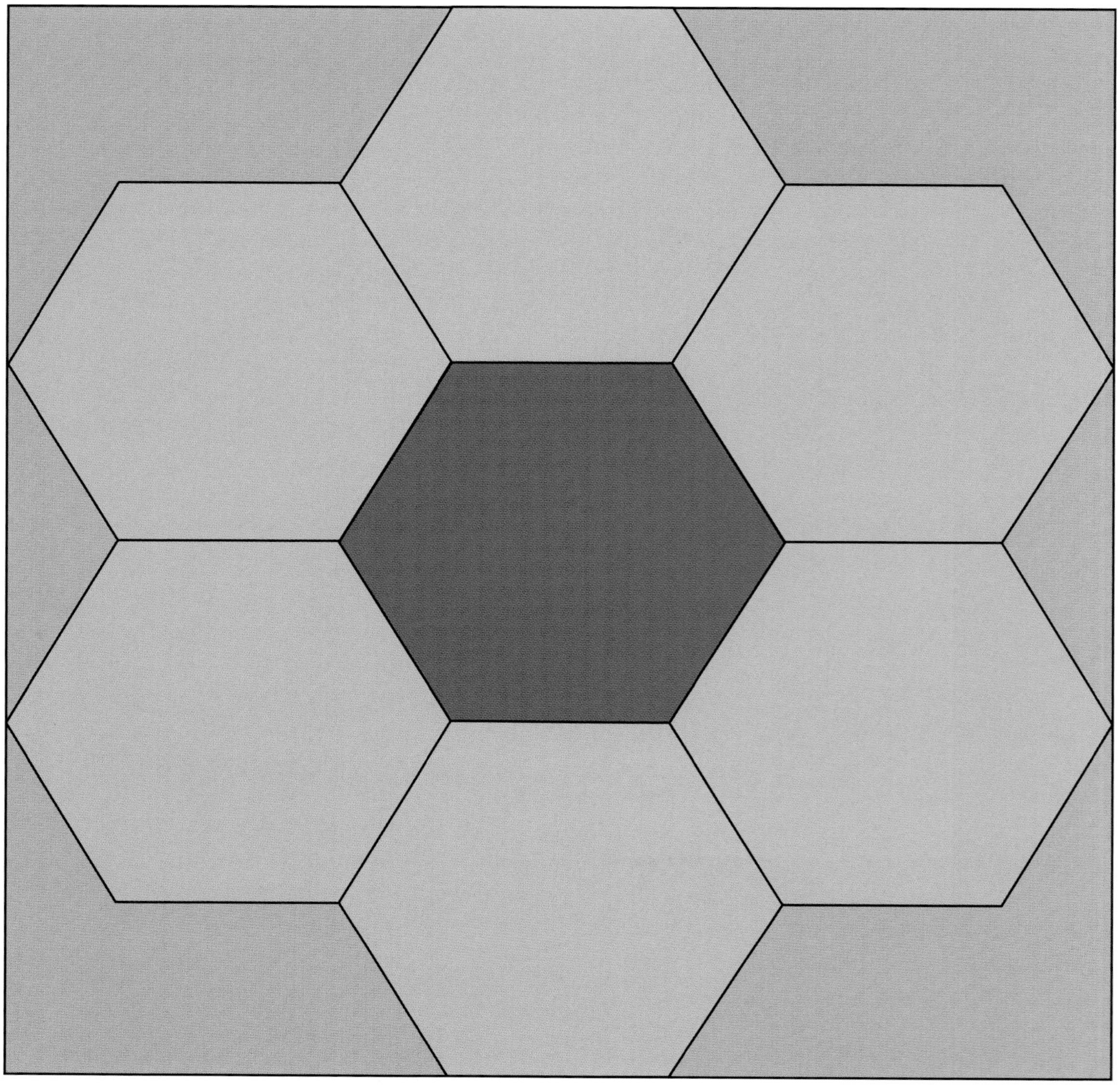

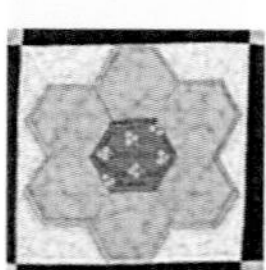

February 20

Dear Friends,

The weather here in Ohio is warming up. Freeman is anxious to get started in the fields. Freeman has been busy helping arrange marriages right now as one of his duties of being a Deacon. The children all seem to be doing well. Katie and Lydiann are playing in the kitchen while the other children are at school.

The boys are really learning a lot about the farm and how to take care of the livestock. Yesterday Freeman showed Nathan how to hitch and unhitch the horses. It didn't take long and now he can do it by himself. David and Ivan have been feeding most of the livestock as well as milking the cows.

Martha has her hexagons all pieced together. She could not wait to show her grandmother. They have sandwiched it together and we will have a family quilting here soon. I have decided that instead of hand piecing my Spider Web quilt, I will use my treadle sewing machine.

*Regina*

# 66. Warm Chickens

February 28

Dear Friends,

I had to sit down tonight and tell you what happened during supper tonight. Little Katie was getting ready to go to the barn to feed the chickens. I told her to wear her boots to keep her feet warm. Soon we were all seated at the table enjoying our meal of fried chicken, mashed potatoes, corn and bread. We all began to hear this little peeping noise. Daniel left the table to see where it was coming from. You can imagine the look on our faces when he came around the corner with little Katie's boots full of little chickens. She thought if her boots would keep her feet warm that they would also keep the baby chickens warm. Daniel took her out to the barn and helped her return the chickens.

I have embroidered some tea towels for all of Daniel's sisters for teaching me how to embroider. They helped me put my Monkey Wrench quilt in the frame last week. I am also surprised at how much Dale has learned about the fundamentals of farming.

Friday I am going over to Fern King's home for a quilting. We are going to work on a quilt for the schoolteacher.

Miriam

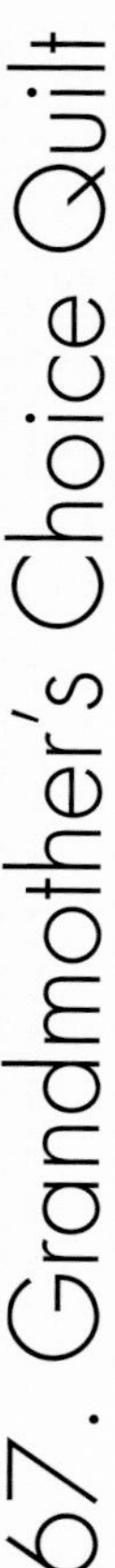

March 8

Dear Friends,

Spring seems to be just around the corner as most of the snow is starting to melt. We're looking forward to the warmer weather and being able to work in the gardens and fields. This morning, I walked to school with my little ones to watch the older children participate in a spelling bee. The scholars did very well and have been studying very hard with their spelling words. Our school is made up of 11 families, which make up the 32 scholars that are in the classroom. The teacher does a very good job in handling all the children.

The school is located on our neighbor, Abner Glick's, farm. His wife, Sadie, and some of the mothers prepared a lunch for all of the children. They thought it was a real treat to be able to leave school and walk to the Glick's home for lunch. Since Abner is such a good storyteller, he told the children a couple stories that he memorized from the "Martyrs' Mirror." The children were soon ready to head back to school.

Last week a few of the neighbors came over and helped me finish my Grandmother's Choice quilt top. I presented the quilt to one of my grandmothers for her 80th birthday. When we were getting ready to leave my grandmother's house, she presented me with a bag of old fabric swatches that she had saved from a traveling salesman. There has to be over 500 different swatches and I'm really not sure what pattern to choose for them. If anyone has any good ideas, please let me know.

*Rachel*

# 68. Maple Syrup

March 15

Dear Friends,

I have good news to share in that our family was blessed with a new son on February 26th who we named Emanuel. He is doing very well and seems to be a very good baby. Family has been here helping with the chores. It is a really busy time for Roy, as he is finishing up with the maple syrup tapping. He has about 3,000 maple trees and is hoping to produce between 700 and 800 gallons. The only problem is that the snow has been deep this winter and spring was colder than usual. Both of these mean that the sap is not flowing very well.

Clara and Katie are doing well and really enjoy school. William spends a lot of his time taking care of Amos. He teaches him how he can help with simple chores like loading the wood box or feeding the animals. It was time tonight for baths. I heated the water on the stove to do the dishes and when the rest of the water was heated, we brought the tub to the kitchen and bath time began. I always open the door of the stove to circulate more heat into the kitchen during these cooler nights. I'll be glad when the weather is warmer and we can use the bathhouse.

My Streak of Lightning quilt is almost finished. Just before Emanuel was born, I hand pieced a Basket quilt. I received the pattern from one of my grandmothers who had made the same quilt many years earlier out of rayons and wools.

# 69. The Quilting

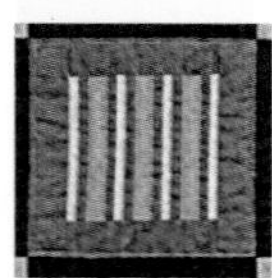

March 28

Dear Friends,

I had some of the neighborhood women over today for a quilting. We're making a quilt for Ida Mae Yutzy who is in our church district and will be moving to Iowa. Their family has bought an old Amish farm. We chose a Bar pattern, as it would be easy to piece together. A few of the older girls not only watched the younger children, but kept our irons heated on the stove. This made our sewing and ironing go very fast. The quilt was in the frame before lunch and was almost finished by supper. Tomorrow the neighbors will return to finish it.

Eli is getting anxious to be out in the fields. He usually waits until the first week of May to plow down the old cornstalks and plant his new crops. If the weather continues to stay this warm, he says he will be able to get an earlier start. He's going with his brother this Saturday to an auction to look at some Belgian horses. He is taking Marlin and Vernon with him. All they have talked about all week is going to see the horses.

*Martha*

# 70. Fruit Roll

April 8

Dear Friends,

The weather here has really improved. Spring has finally arrived. We have been so busy getting ready for the planting season. The children and I are enjoying being outdoors more. Lyle has been putting in longer days and is mighty hungry by suppertime. We cannot wait for the fresh vegetables to bloom in the garden.

We went to visit Henry at school today because they were celebrating his teacher's birthday. They had a fruit roll for their teacher. She told the children to get out their lunches and as they did, they also began to roll their fruit up to the front of the room. There were plenty of oranges, apples and even a few honeydew melons. Some of the children even brought fruit cocktail in cans. The mothers took some of the fruit and made all the children a fruit salad for dessert. The teacher did not think anyone knew it was her birthday.

After lunch, some English tourists came to visit the school. They seemed like very nice people, but had to be told to put their cameras away. They would not stop taking photographs of the children or the teacher. I wish the English understood our ways.

Rebecca

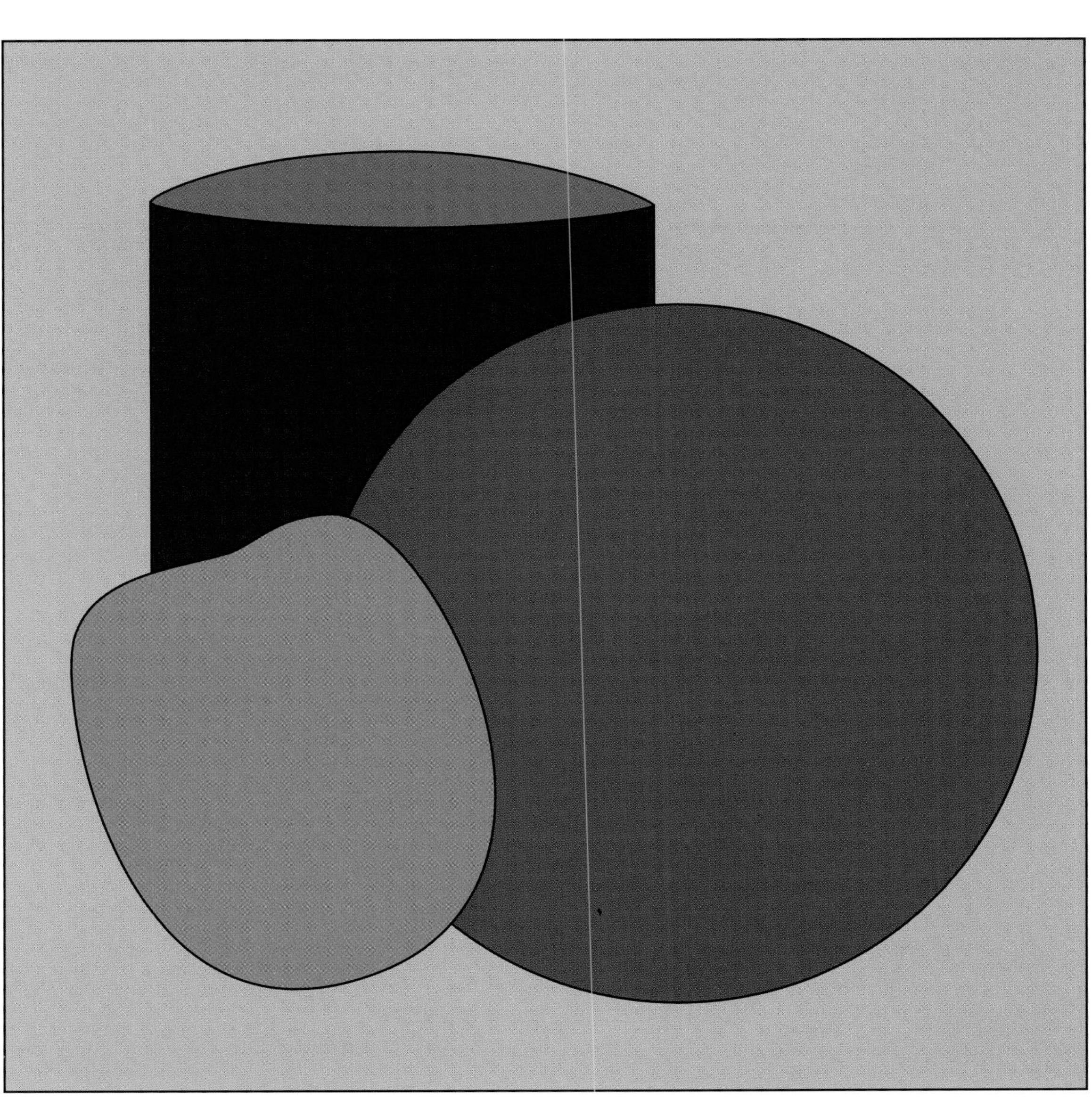

# 71. Jacob's Ladder

April 17

Dear Friends,

Our family is doing very well and they're also very busy getting ready for the planting season. The older children will be going to school only half-days the next two weeks so they can come home early and help us with the many chores this season brings.

Rachel, have you thought about taking those fabric swatches from the traveling salesman and just making a One-Patch quilt? That way you would not have to cut the old fabrics up. I had to go to town today to pick up a few things. I went to the hardware store and bought a new belt for my treadle sewing machine, as it broke yesterday. I also purchased some denim to make the boys some new pants and some blue chambray for their new work shirts. Their cotton fabrics were also on sale, so I purchased some solid colors to work on a Center Diamond quilt. My Jacob's Ladder quilt is almost finished.

I am really looking forward to having our reunion at our home this August. I really would like all of us to work on the Center Diamond quilt that I will be stitching together. Well, it has been nice catching up on all of your lives, but it is now time to get back to my chores.

# 72. Softball Game

April 30

Dear Friends,

God has blessed us with a healthy child who we named Gideon. The older children and our families have been such a big help. Martha was here visiting already with some of her vegetable soup and a Log Cabin quilt that she made for Gideon.

The children finished school today with their annual picnic. We spent the afternoon visiting and had a nice lunch with homemade noodles, corn fritters and watercress sandwiches. The fathers and sons had their yearly softball game. Two of the fathers went home with sprained ankles. Naomi cannot wait until she is old enough for school. Their teacher is Wilma King. She is 17 years old and is going to be returning next year.

Melvin and Elvin are such a big help on the farm that Leroy is going to take them to an auction this Saturday. He is looking into buying 20 more dairy cows to add to our herd.

Edna

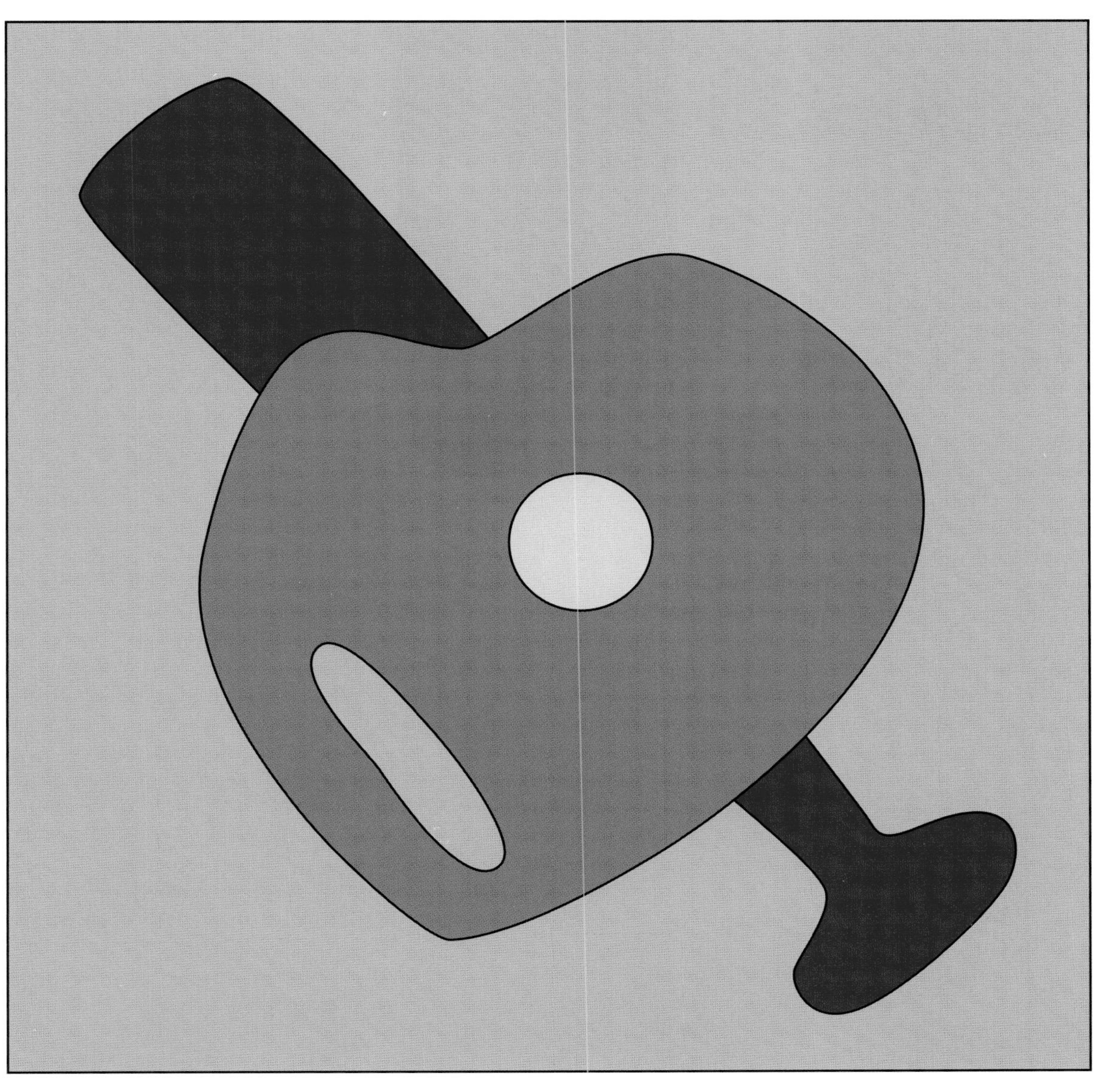

# 73. Bathhouse

May 6

Dear Friends,

It is a beautiful spring morning. I'm sitting in the backyard at my picnic table writing you a letter. Marvin and the boys are all in the field. This spring they bought a new horse-drawn hay baler so they no longer have to gather the loose hay by hand. Marvin guides the team and Timothy and Joseph take the bales and move them to the front of the wagon. Edith is gathering the eggs in the chicken coop. Little Wilma is taking a morning nap.

Martin's sisters and I are going over to Anna Troyers' home this afternoon to do some cleaning and baking. She was kicked by one of the workhorses and has a broken leg. Most of her family lives in another district, so we're going to help out until some of her family members arrive here. We have hired an English van driver to drive us today because a big storm is moving our way this afternoon.

Well, I must close for now, as there are chores to be done. The weather has been warm enough now that it is time to clean out the bathhouse. It will be nice again to take a bath in the bathhouse instead of filling up the tub in the kitchen.

# 74. Shetland Pony

May 10

Dear Friends,

What a good time we had here today. We had a family reunion at our home with 84 in attendance. All of my brothers and sisters were able to attend. Even my sister, who lives in Iowa, was able to attend. It has been a while since we've all been together. We had so much fun visiting.

Dan had a big surprise for all the children. Last week when he was at a horse auction, he bought a small Shetland pony. The children took turns riding him most of the day. They almost did not want to stop for lunch. We all had to laugh when little Elis wanted to hook the pony up to the buggy. The older children played tag and hide-and-seek.

My oldest sister, Lizzie, gave all of us sisters a set of Double Nine-Patch blocks. She had hand pieced them using some of our old clothes that she found in my mother's attic. What a wonderful surprise. Supper was soon finished and our day was over. We ended the night singing some of our favorite hymns and had popcorn and lemonade before everyone headed home.

Lavern

# 75. Diagonal Triangles

May 26

Dear Friends,

As I'm starting to write my letter, I am thinking about the verse from Proverbs 27:1, "Do not boast about tomorrow, for you do not know what a day may bring forth." Today started out like any other normal day. The morning chores were finished and Abe headed out to the furniture shop with the boys to work on some of his projects. It was not 10 minutes later when Eugene came running and yelling out of the barn. Simon had stepped in the way of the saw and was hurt badly.

I sent Mary down to the phone booth to call for help. The emergency vehicles were soon here to help us. They took him to the hospital for some stitches and he will need some time to mend. By the time we arrived back home, the neighbors had finished our evening chores and had our dinner ready.

# 76. Shelling Peas

June 5

Dear Friends,

We have been experiencing some really hot weather already this summer in Ohio. The fields are beginning to become dry and could really use a good rainstorm.

I have spent most of the week with the children, picking the peas in the garden. The best part is sitting down in the shade and shelling them. It is a good time for me to share some of my favorite Bible stories or sing the children's favorite hymns. It seems to make the work go much faster when we work as a family to get the farming done.

I went to a quilting on Tuesday. We worked on a quilt for one of the overseas relief sales. It was a Lady of the Lake pattern. It has a lot of pieces, but I'm going to try to use some of my scraps to make one. We had a couple of family quiltings here and Martha's Hexagon quilt is all quilted. It is her first finished quilt. It was nice to have three generations working on her Hexagon quilt.

*Regina*

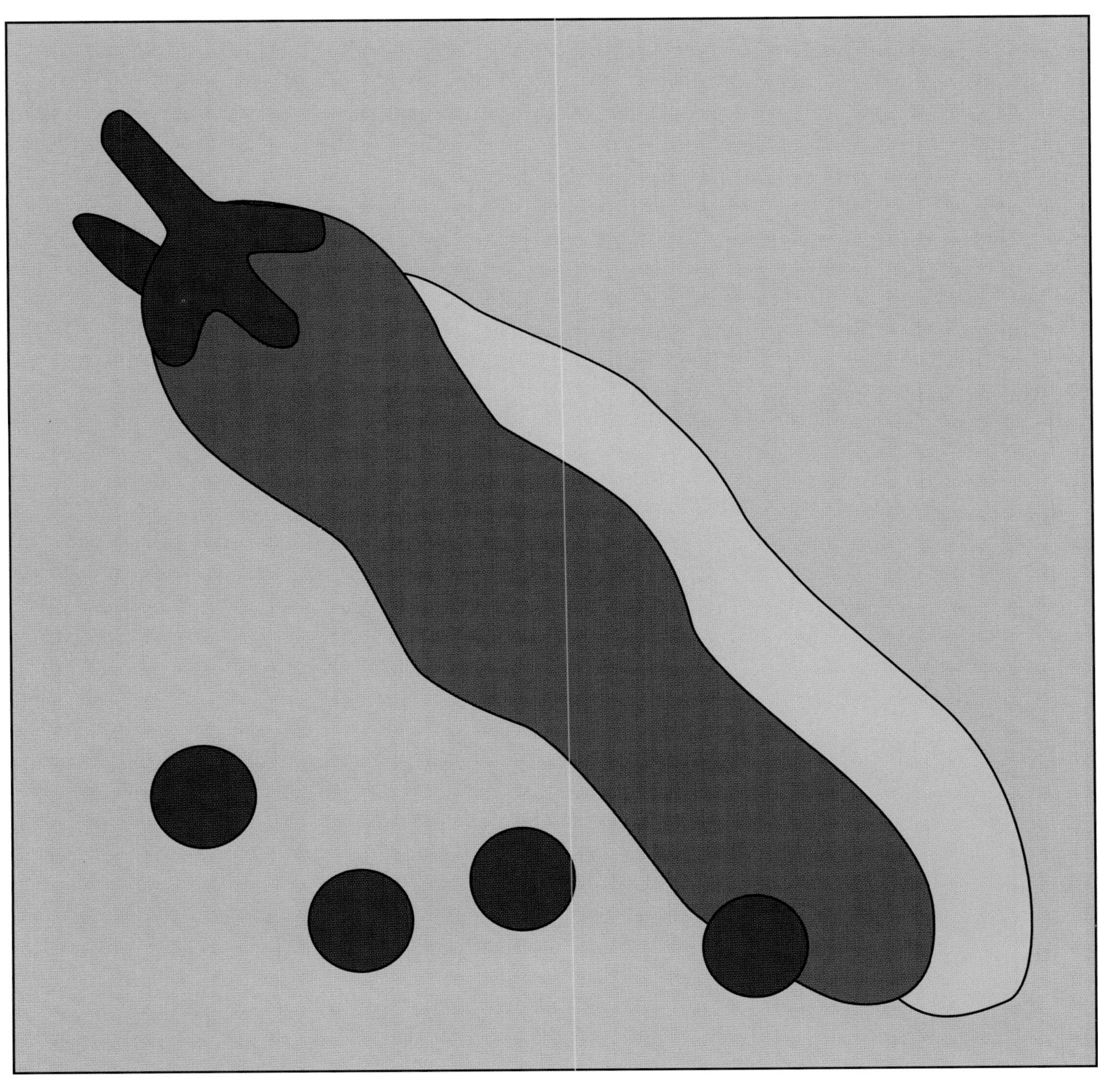

# 77. Monkey Wrench

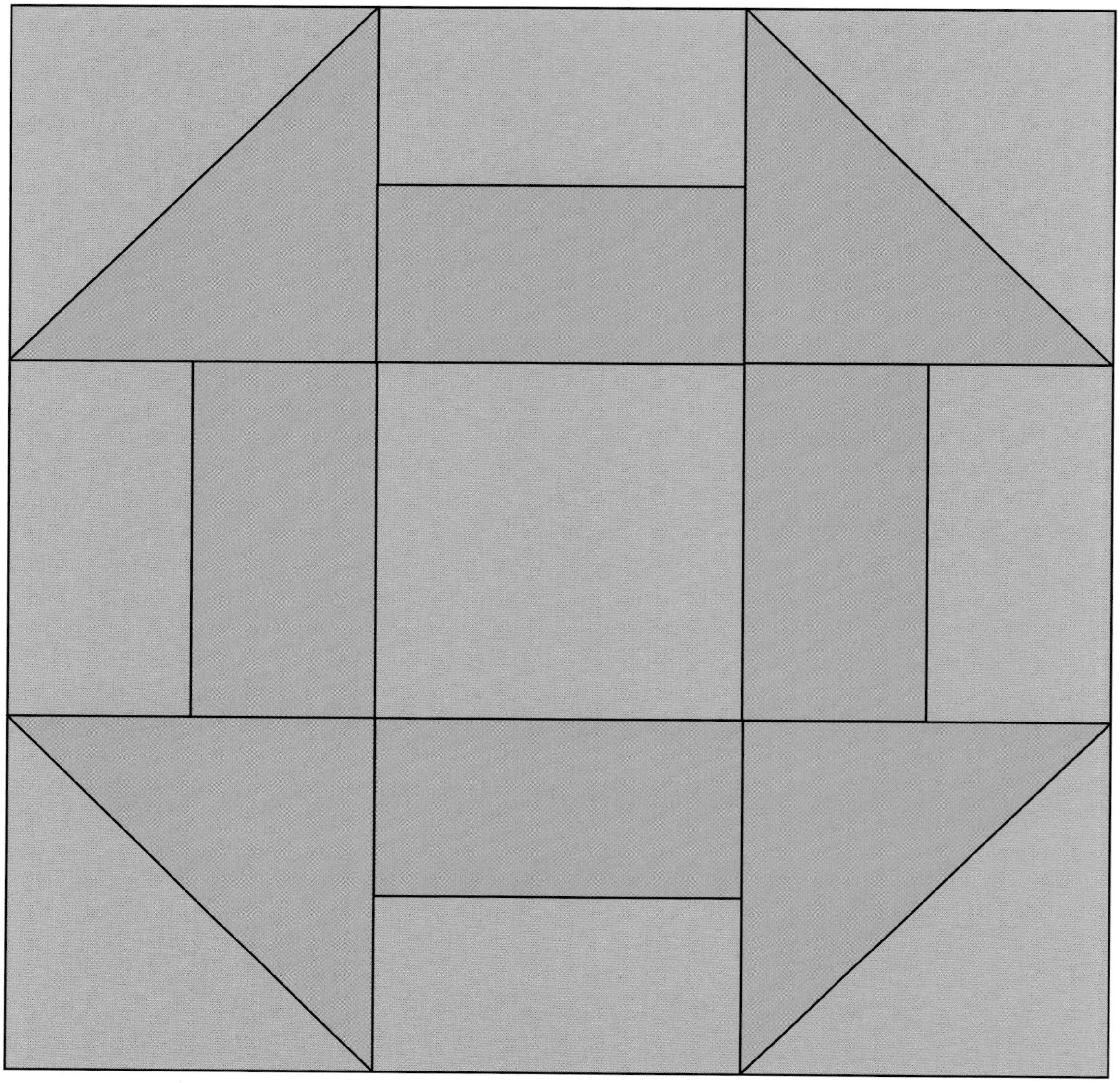

June 17

Dear Friends,

Today we went to the train station to pick up Daniel's aunt who will be visiting at our home for a few weeks. She lives in a district in Canada and her name is Kathy Schwartz. The bishop of her district only allows travel by buggy or train to visit a relative. They are not allowed to ride bicycles at all because they feel it offers too much mobility. She presented us with a Nine-Patch quilt that was made by Daniel's great-grandmother. It had been put away in a chest and was never used. The fabrics are very old, but are in very good condition.

I have finished quilting my Monkey Wrench quilt. I will probably wait until fall to start on another project. I'm thinking of doing a crazy quilt using some of the stitches that Daniel's sisters have taught me.

The children are doing very well and Daniel has been very busy with his bishop duties and farm work.

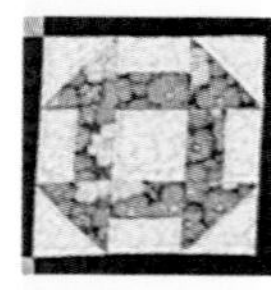

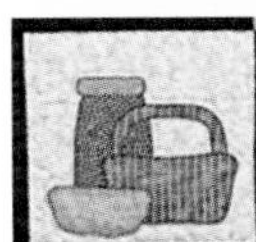



June 28

Dear Friends,

We're all doing well here. It was almost 90 degrees this afternoon, so I am enjoying the cool breeze the night has brought. It has been a long day and I am enjoying reading the circle letter now that the children are all in bed.

Lavina, I liked your idea of using the traveling salesman's swatches and making a quilt using the simple One-Patch pattern. I have had the older children mark the squares and cut them out. The original samples were cut with pinking shears, so they all needed trimming. I have been piecing them together on my treadle sewing machine instead of by hand because some of the fabrics are so old and delicate.

Tonight we all went to the haystack supper held to benefit Samuel Bontrager, who is the father of six children in our district. The money will go to help pay some of his medical bills after his accident at the sawmill. It was fun to watch the children make their haystacks with corn chips on the bottom, topped with hamburger, vegetables and cheese. The final topping was some homemade salsa. My neighbor, Fannie Schlabach, and I canned 56 quarts of salsa for the supper. We had so much fun making it and it was a good way to use up the tomatoes.

*Rachel*

# 79. Roof Frolic

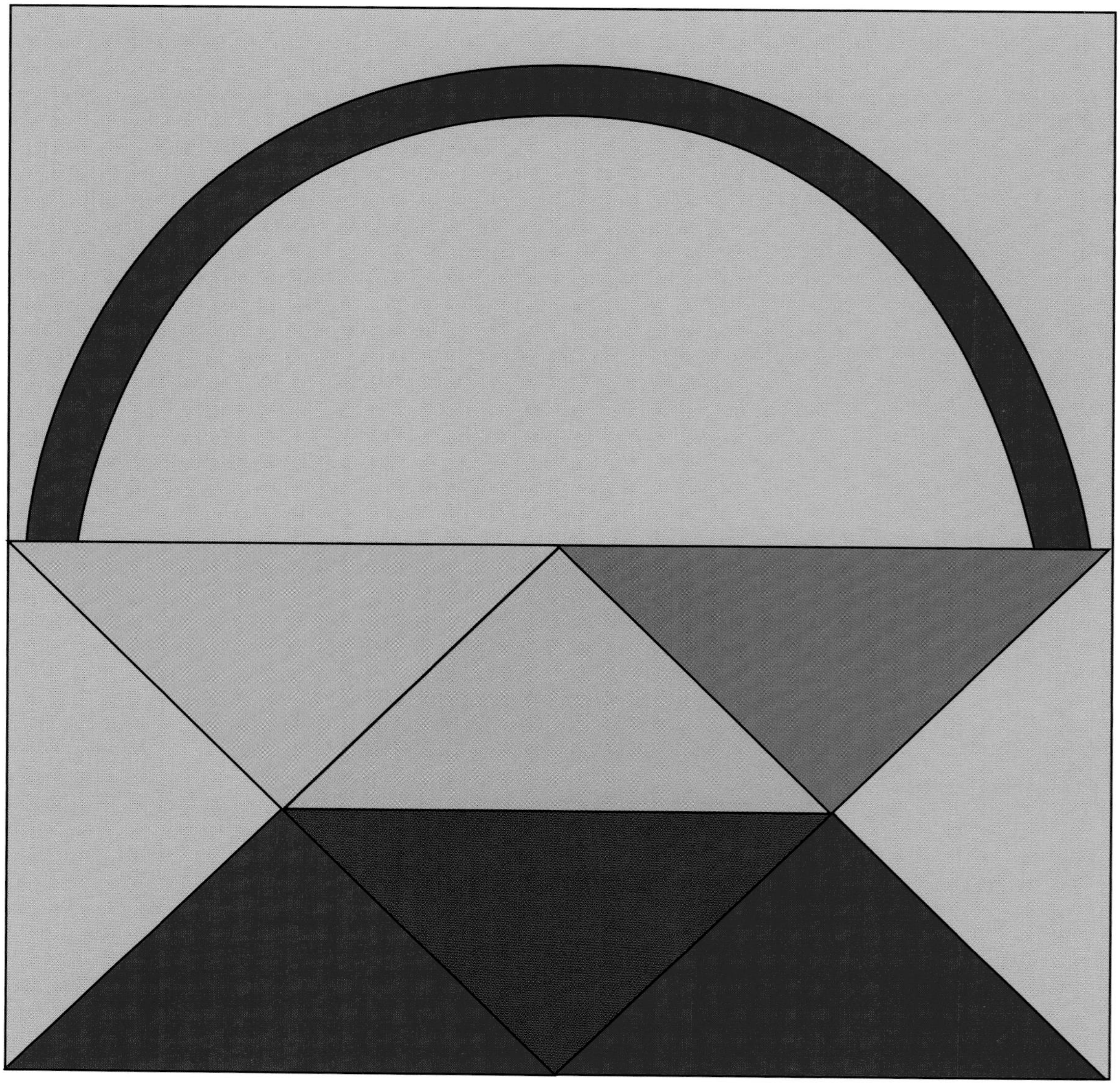

July 7

Dear Friends,

The children seem to be growing so fast. Little Emanuel is such an active baby. I have finally finished hand quilting his little Basket quilt. Roy has hired one of Joe Slabaugh's daughters for this summer to help with the chores and the children. Her name is Erla and she is a very good worker.

On Saturday, Roy and his brothers went to Stephen Luthy's home for a roof frolic. The top of his barn was destroyed last week by a tornado. Some of the older boys went along and were given easier jobs to help out where they could. All of the other family members arrived later for supper. There was plenty of chicken, vegetables, potatoes and fresh bread for all. The women brought all kinds of pies, from peanut butter to raisin to chocolate fudge. Of course, shoofly and apple pie were the most popular. The men finished not only the roof, but also most of the pie. Most of the children preferred the doughnuts. We ended the night with a singing.

Lydiann

# 80. Laundry Machine

July 19

Dear Friends,

It has been an interesting morning so far. I had taken some hot water from the burning stove and put it in the washtub to begin my laundry. Our cat was very interested in what I was doing. As I was turning the hand-lever for the wash machine to agitate the water, he decided to jump and landed in the tub. After drying him off, I thought for sure that he would stay away. I then began to run the clothing through the rollers to squeeze out the water and, all of a sudden, realized that his tail was going through, too. He seemed fine and did not come near the washing machine the rest of the day. Barbara and Aden did not want to come near the machine either. I finally got the laundry ready to hang outside. Our clothesline is on a pulley that runs from the kitchen door to the chicken coop. I had half of the laundry on the line and it broke. Eli came in from the fields and helped me fix it and gather the laundry to be washed again. I began to wonder what kind of day this would be since lunchtime was still an hour away.

The mail arrived and inside was the circle letter. I had to take a break and tell you about my morning adventure. That is why I have enclosed a sketch of my laundry machine with my circle letter. Well, it is time to get back to my chores and get lunch ready for the children and Eli. I'm going to be making cabbage soup, blueberry muffins and rhubarb pie.

*Martha*

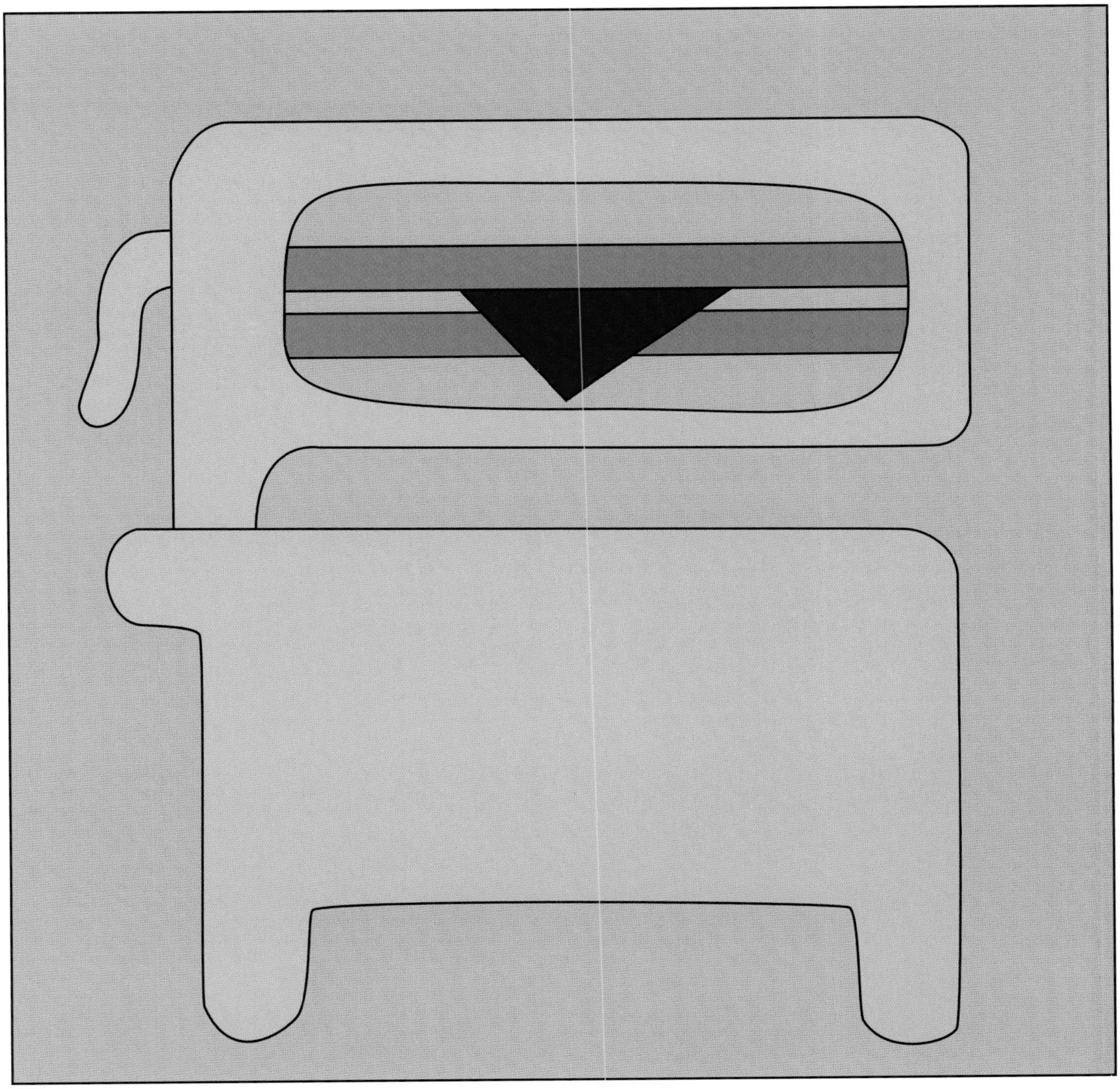

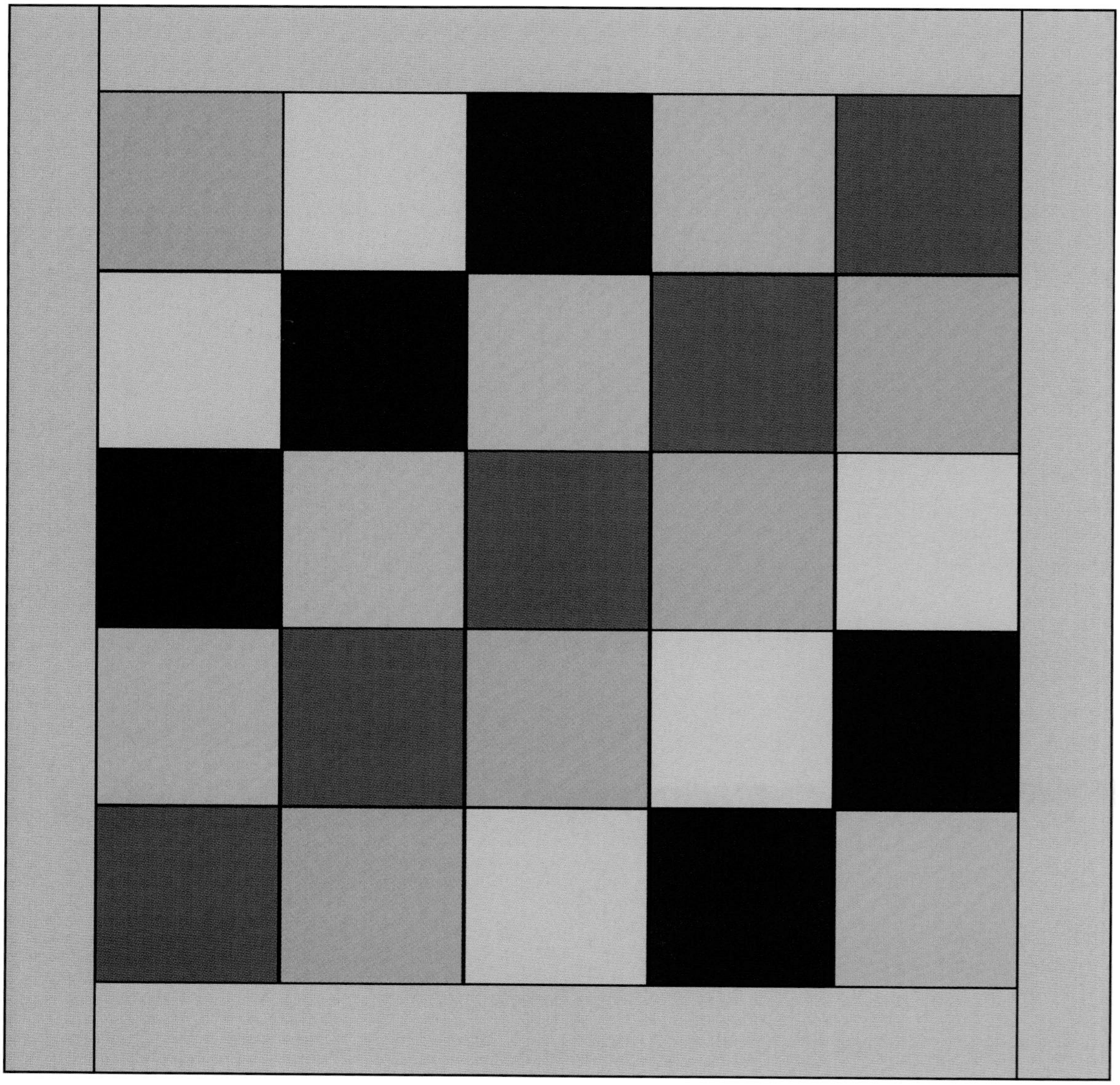

# 81. Diagonal Patches

July 29

Dear Friends,

Our new daughter, Sadie, who is almost two months old now is doing very well. We named her after Lyle's grandmother. The grandmothers were here today with some fabrics and brown paper. I had them trace some old patterns of mine onto the brown paper to make new patterns for some new dresses for Sadie. They soon had three new dresses finished for her and then began to check out my latest quilting project.

They took the squares that I had left from my Sunshine and Shadow quilt and placed them so they formed rows of the same fabric going diagonally. I prepared supper while they sewed it together and they soon had it tied with Sadie sitting and playing on top of it. I will bring it with me, with a few of my other projects, when we come to the reunion next week.

Lyle soon returned home with Henry and the grandfathers, who were at a machinery auction. They felt that they had a very good day because they were able to buy a new corn binder without rubber wheels on it. One of the rules of our district is that we cannot have any farm implement with rubber tires.

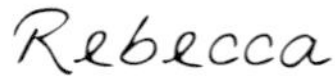

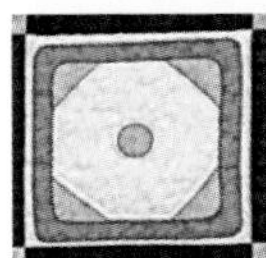



August 8

Dear Friends,

Things are returning back to normal after the last couple of days that we spent visiting each other at our home. I really enjoyed you quilting on my Center Diamond quilt and it was nice to have the older girls to take care of the younger children and help us quilt at the frame. It is so nice that we're able to pass down our quilting from generation to generation .

The boys really enjoyed playing corner ball. I could not tell if they enjoyed throwing the ball or dodging the ball more. I sent a sketch of the corner ball field for my block this time. The younger boys had so much fun making believe they were taking buggy trips to the horse auction, using the twine as their reins. The girls spent most of their time working on their quilt blocks.

Lavina

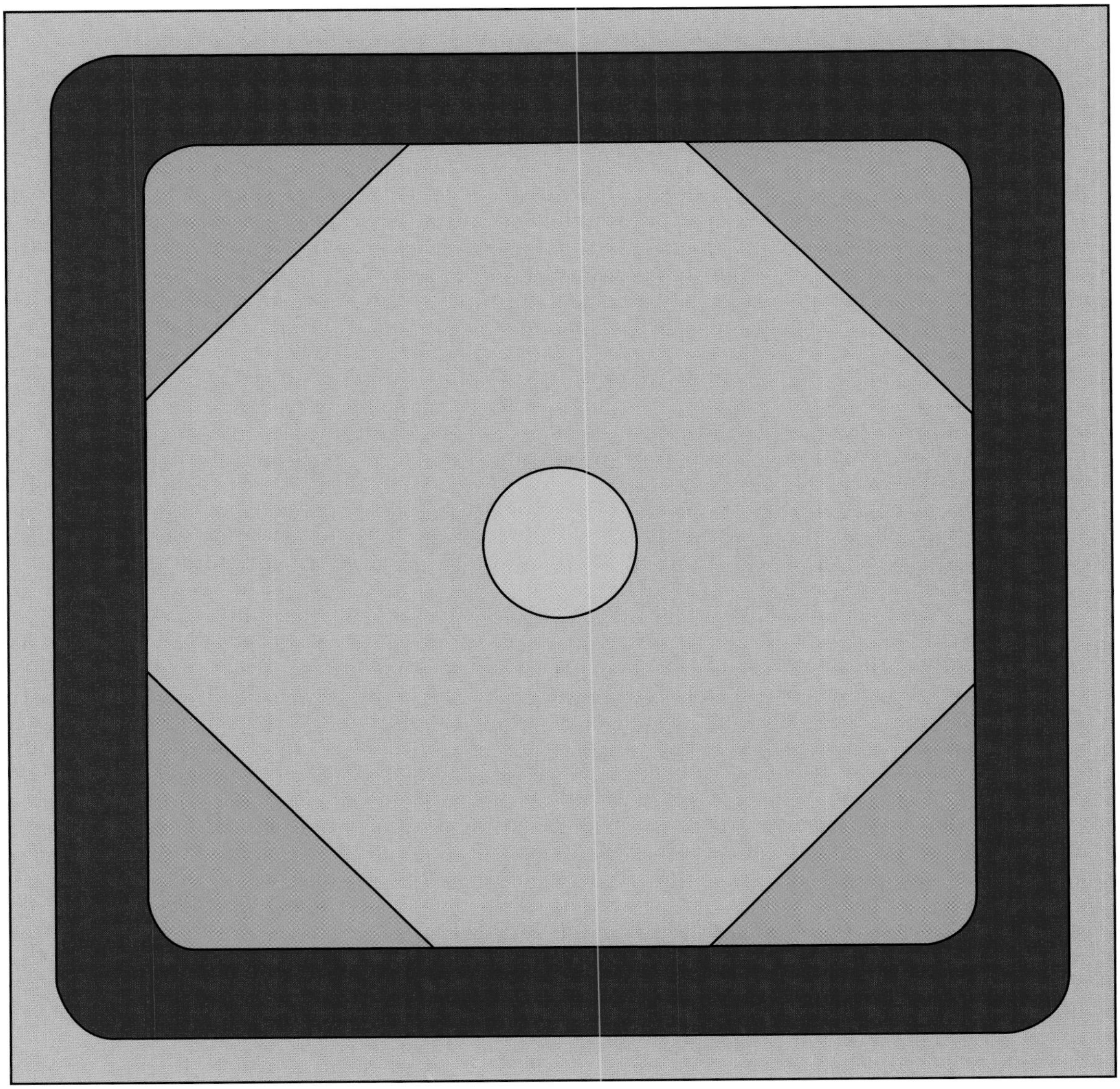

# 83. Irish Chain

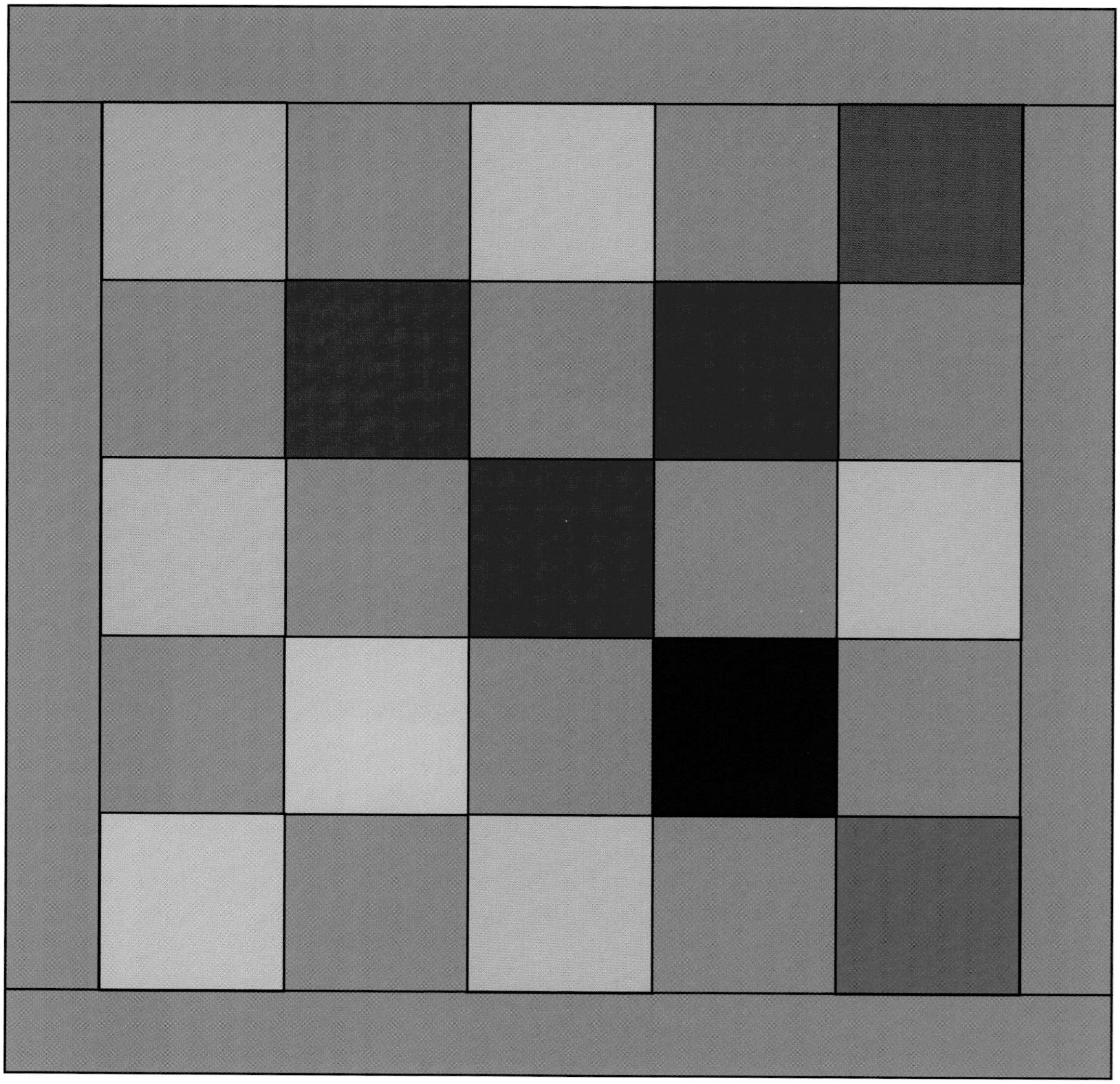

August 17

Dear Friends,

It is hard to believe that summer is almost over. Saturday we had a picnic with some of our neighbors after the daily chores were finished. Some of the men and boys enjoyed a quick swim in the pond before supper. For supper we had fried chicken, noodle casserole, fresh green beans and numerous desserts. We ended the night singing hymns by the pond. Naomi thought that the frogs and crickets were singing right along with us.

School will be starting in two weeks. The first two weeks of school Elvin and Melvin will only be going to school half-days because Leroy will be needing their help on the farm. He wants to get some of the fields harvested, as we are expecting a cooler fall season.

I am looking forward to the cooler season because I sure do get more quilting finished. The first project that I'm going to try to finish sewing together is the Irish Chain I have been working on. My sister is having a get-together on Friday. We all have to bring our sack lunches and 3" squares. We're going to be working on a quilt for our school auction in two weeks.

Edna

September 3

Dear Friends,

Our family has been doing very well. We have been getting the farm ready for the cooler weather. It is quiet during the day here now that school has started. Wilma misses the children when they leave for school. Her face really lights up when one of Marvin's sisters stops over with her children.

We have been very busy working at the school. Marvin has been appointed the school custodian this year. He is in charge of making sure that all repairs and chores are done at the school. The last two Saturdays we have had work days for all of the families that are in our church district. We whitewashed the outside of the schoolhouse and cleaned up the playground. Marvin made a weekly schedule of the families that are in charge of bringing the wood to school to keep the stove going.

Marvin's sisters and I get together at least once a week to work on our quilting projects. The men and children enjoy this because afterwards we all have a family dinner together. I am working on a Courthouse Steps quilt top and have almost all of the blocks pieced together. Marvin's oldest sister has a daughter who will be getting married next week and she has 14 finished quilts in her hope chest.

*Frieda*

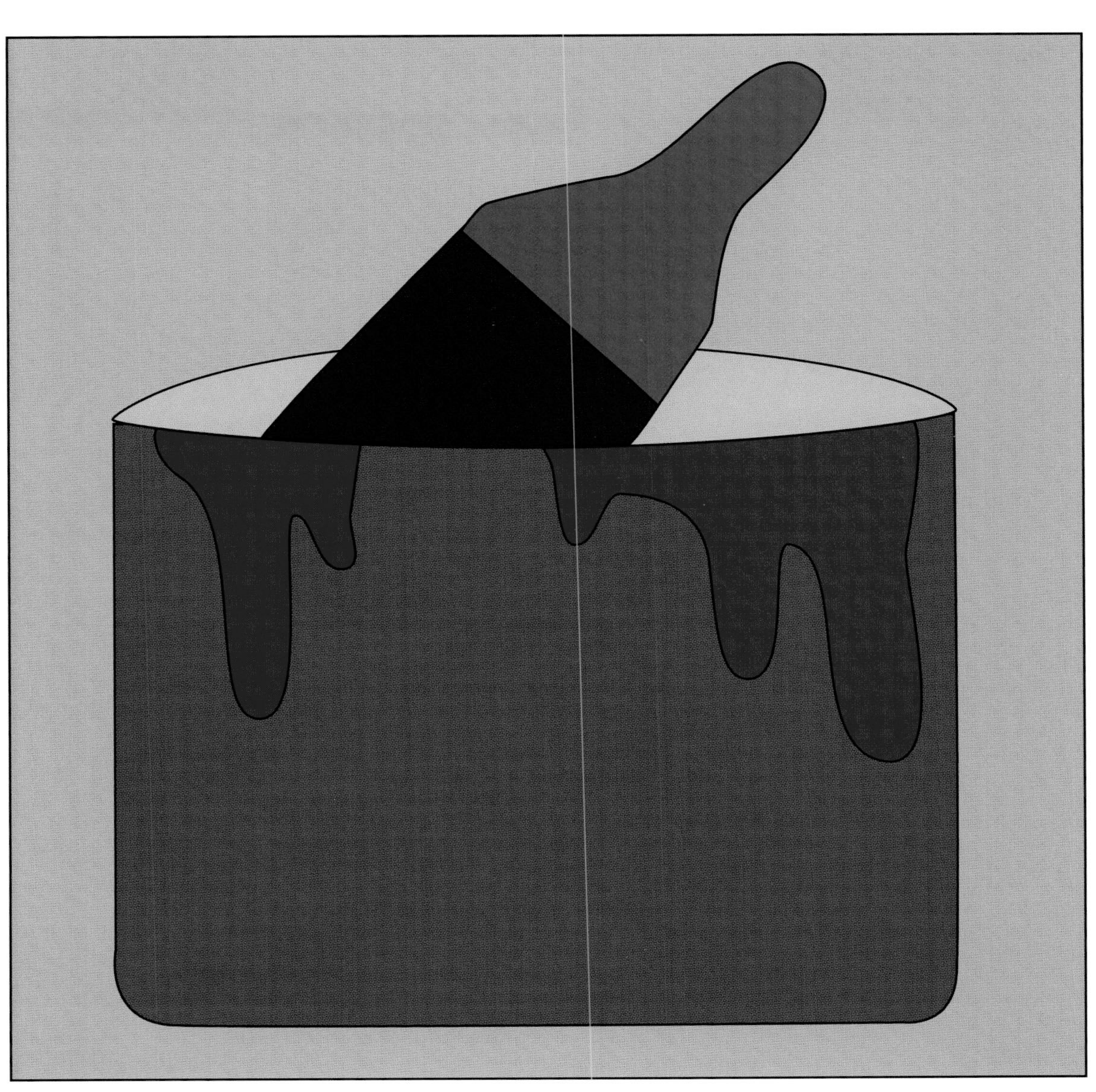

# 85. Star in a Star

September 12

Dear Friends,

Life was to change for our family on September 6th. This started out as a normal day getting the chores finished and all having breakfast together. Dan and Joseph drove the buggy to town to get some supplies. They had been gone about 15 minutes when a neighbor from down the road appeared in my drive. He said there had been an accident and a car had hit the buggy from behind. Dan's mother watched the children as I went with the neighbor to the accident.

The ambulance arrived to take them to the hospital. When we arrived at the hospital, I found out that they both had died instantly. I know it all was for a reason and that God makes no mistakes. I know that with God's grace, he will help me get through every day. The block that I have enclosed is a Star in a Star, the outer star to represent Dan and the inner star to represent Joseph. Job 1:21.

Lavern

# 86. Cornhusking Event

September 21

Dear Friends,

It has been good to see so many of our families helping out at Lavern's this past week. The support from family and friends is so important at a time like this. We appreciated your support so much when Simon was injured in the sawmill accident.

I have been busy doing a lot of canning this past week. We have a few elderly neighbors that are no longer able to can, so they bring over their vegetables and I can their vegetables for them. They, in turn, let me keep some of the vegetables that I canned. This seems to work out for all of our families. It is also a good way for us to help our elderly neighbors.

On Friday night we went to watch the youth event at Lamar Stolzfoos' home. They had a cornhusking event for the young people in our church district. The boys chose a girl to pair off with and then began to shuck corn. The boys rapidly took the corn from the stalks and the girls shucked it as fast as they could. Benjamin Mast and Anna Yoder were the fastest couple. The young people really enjoy the event and it is a good way to get your corn shucked. The end of the night came soon with popcorn and lemonade and soon the buggies began to head home.

*Ida*

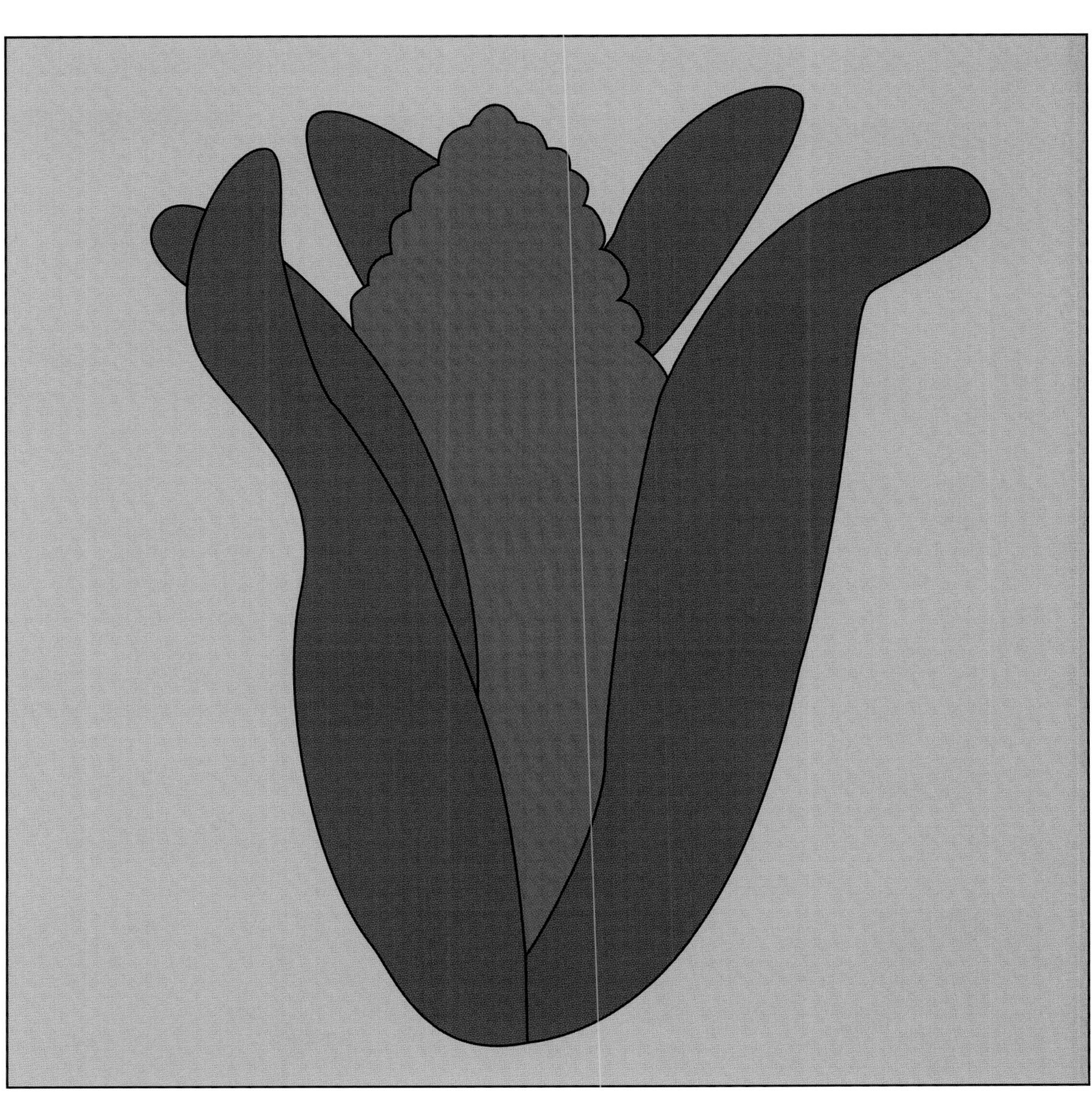

# 87. Lady of the Lake

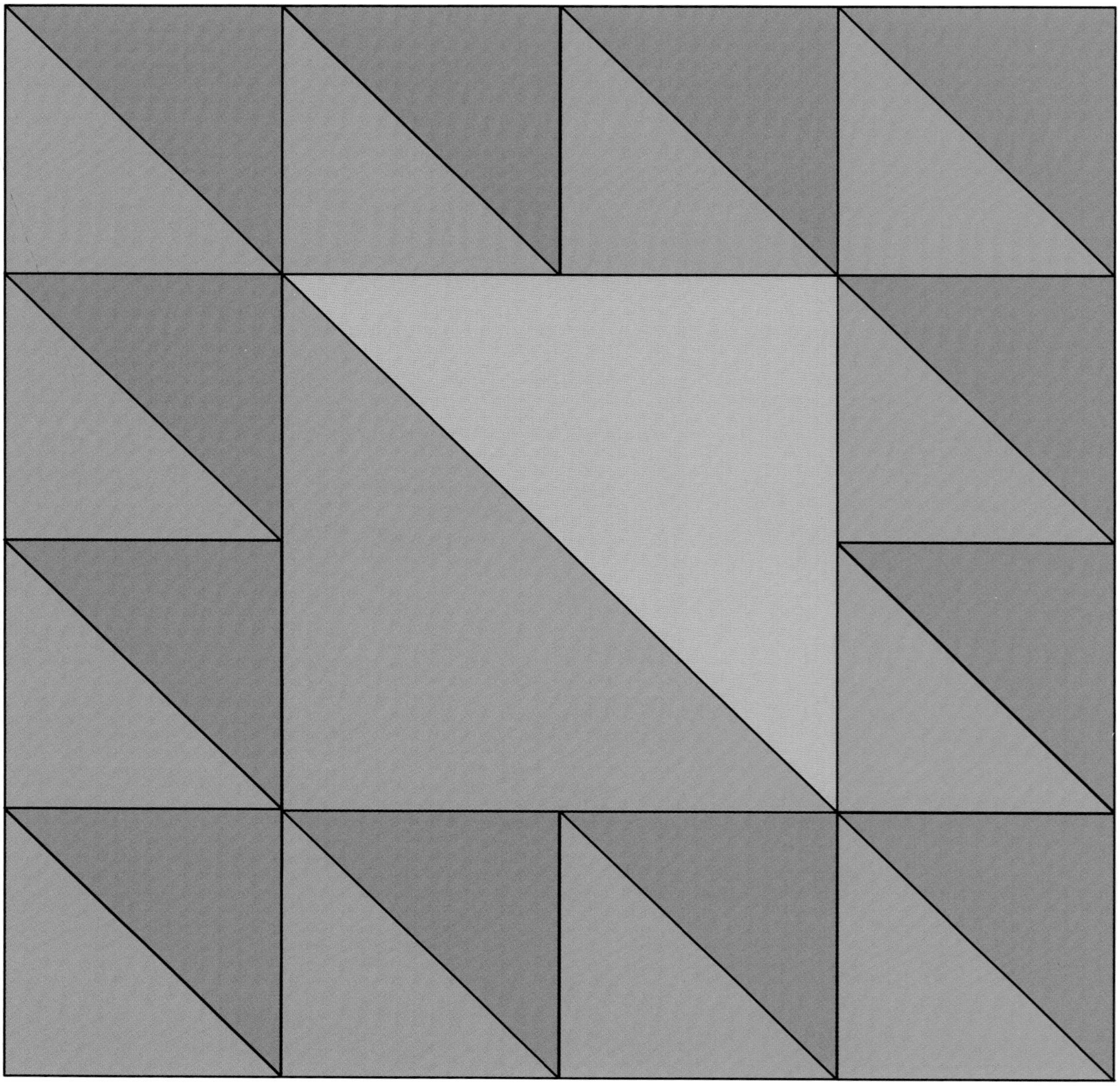

September 30

Dear Friends,

It is Sunday afternoon and I am reading this circle letter as Freeman is reading the weekly newspaper. He just finished reading the children some stories from the "Martyr's Mirror." They are so interested in the old stories about their ancestors. They are now in the kitchen playing board games.

It has been a busy week finishing up with the alfalfa. There'll be more time now during the day, as I will not have to cook for the alfalfa threshing crew. The fields are ready for next year and the local neighbors that we hired have returned to their jobs at the furniture and harness shop. Freeman will be very busy arranging marriages in the next month as part of his deacon duties.

I have started working on my Lady of the Lake quilt using the same pattern as the one we finished this summer for the relief sale. My Spider Web quilt top is on the frame and it is about half finished. I seem to be having a lot of trouble quilting through all the seams. Martha is working on a Center Diamond top because she would like to learn how to quilt feather designs.

*Regina*

October 9

Dear Friends,

We have good news to share with all of you in that we were blessed with a new addition to our family. Charlene was born on September 28th. We chose that name because it is the name of my mother. The children love having a little one in the house. Yesterday, little Katie was sitting with her hoop, practicing her embroidery stitches and explaining them to Charlene.

On Saturday, some members from our church district had a fall harvest picnic. We met at Norman Whetstone's farm and began the morning by making apple cider. Some of the men helped Norman cut wood for his woodpile. Since the schoolhouse is on his property, the children spent their time playing on swing sets and teeter totters. Some of the older children got involved in a volleyball game. It was soon time for lunch with 86 of us in attendance. The women had all planned a surprise for the older children. After lunch, we had a taffy pull and had a very good time stretching the taffy and then wrapping it up. Of course, most of the taffy was eaten before it was wrapped.

Miriam

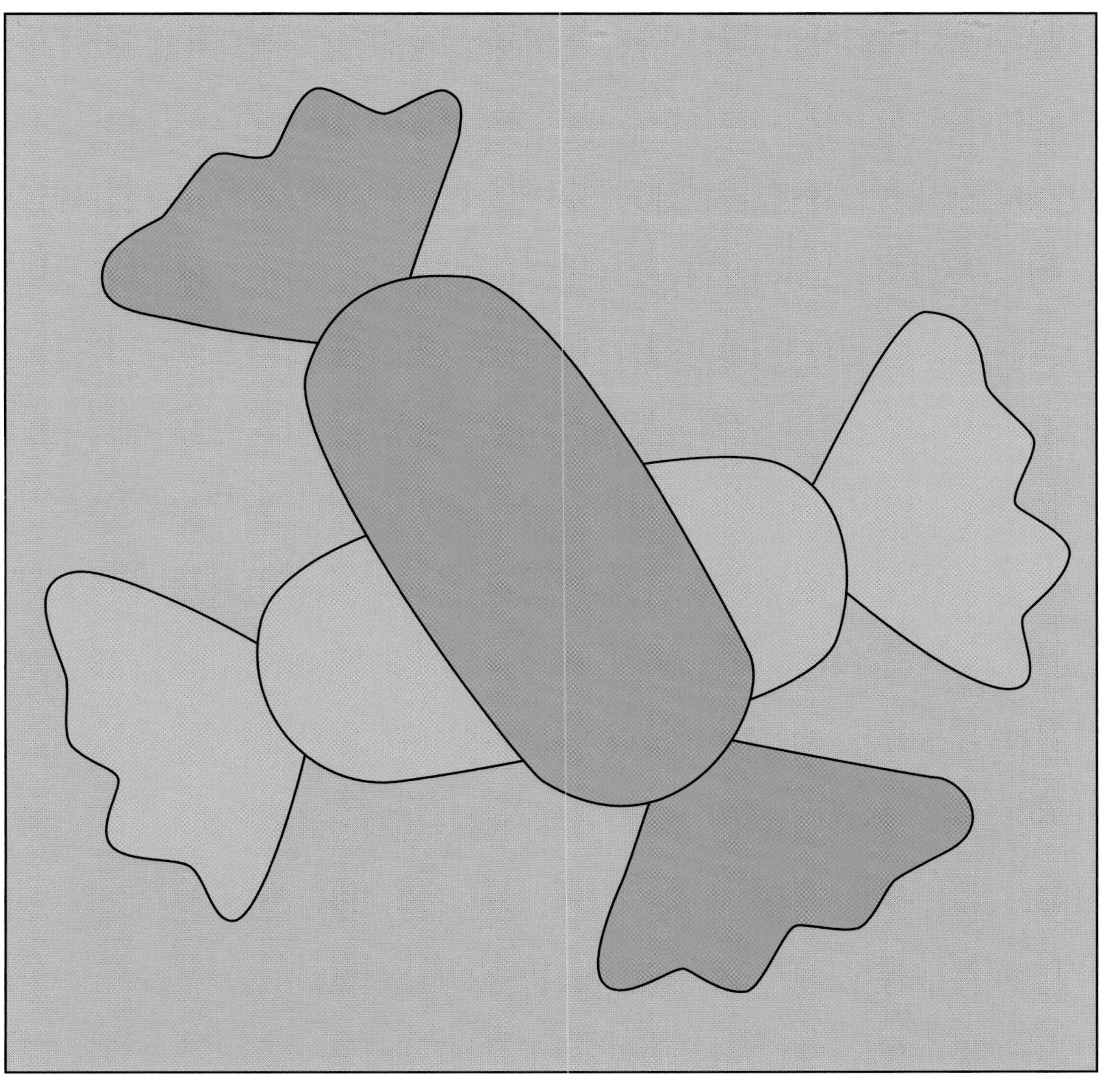

# 89. Center Diamond

October 19

Dear Friends,

The circle letter arrived today with three wedding invitations. Samuel's youngest brother and two cousins are to marry this month and a quilting frolic has been scheduled for all of them. We're going to be making a Center Diamond quilt for all three of them. It will be so nice to be sitting at the frame quilting with all the generations of his family, from his grandmother to some of the younger cousins. We also are going to be spending the afternoon tomorrow cleaning the house that Samuel's youngest brother will be moving into. All the family will be gathered together to do this, so we should be finished in no time at all.

Samuel and the children are doing well and the field work is starting to slow down some. Samuel has been spending most of his time making sure the hay is well stocked for the winter because that is the most important crop that we need for the animals. The girls and I have been doing some extra baking and have been selling some baked goods from our home. On Wednesday we also take some baked goods to two of the local grocers to sell.

*Rachel*

# 90. Missing Puzzle Piece

October 29

Dear Friends,

We gathered together at Betty Erb's home today to work on a quilt for the school auction. There were 20 of us in attendance, along with our small children. We all brought our own sack lunch to make things easier for our hostess. Some of the older girls kept the children busy working on jigsaw puzzles and playing with a wooden farm set. Betty has a large frame that extends down from the ceiling, which is nice because all 20 of us could be seated around the frame. It was fun to share stories and laughter. We all had to laugh when we were almost to the middle of the quilt because we found a missing jigsaw puzzle piece. Somehow the puzzle piece must have fallen on to the batting and was sandwiched in between the layers and nobody noticed it.

Roy and I spent some time on Sunday looking through gardening catalogs, trying to pick out what we would enjoy growing next year. He always says as long as I grow some butternut squash, which is his favorite, I can choose any flowers to border the gardens. The children also like to sit and look through the catalogs to pick out their favorite vegetables.

# 91. Roman Stripes Variation

November 14

Dear Friends,

The corn field is ready for next year and Eli has been spending most of his time in the barn repairing machinery for next season. The children are all well and Marlin and Vernon seem to be enjoying this school year. They cannot wait, however, to get home to take care of the chickens. We are considering building another chicken coop and adding more chickens this spring. We have been selling some of the eggs at the local farmers' market and a few of the local grocery shops. We have had another grocer's store ask us to supply them with eggs, but we cannot keep up with the demand. The boys are really excited about the possibility of taking care of more chickens.

I am enjoying the cool weather and finding more time to work on some of my quilt projects. I have chosen to work on a Roman Stripes variation. It's something a little different from the one that my mother made. It is a good way to use up some old scraps.

One of our English neighbors has asked me if I would be willing to prepare a meal for some tourists that will be visiting her next week. They would like to learn more about the Amish life and eat in an Amish home. She has chosen the menu of fried chicken, mashed potatoes, corn and biscuits. For dessert I'm going to be serving pumpkin and shoofly pie. She was really surprised to learn that shoofly pie was made with brown sugar and molasses. I hope this goes well, as I have never tried anything like this before.

*Martha*

# 92. Storing Eggs

November 21

Dear Friends,

Henry seems to be just like Marlin and Vernon in that he enjoys taking care of the chickens. He is up first thing in the morning feeding them, and by the time he returns home from school, they are out in the chicken coop clucking and waiting for their feed again. We have collected so many eggs lately and have been storing them in the cellar. Henry and I coat the eggs with petroleum jelly to keep in the flavor. We can store them in the cellar until spring. Andy helps Lyle with the dairy cows and the other animals. He has been pecked by the chickens, so he prefers working in the barn with the other animals.

We will be heading off to Iowa next week for a family reunion. We're going to be traveling with an English neighbor who is driving us there in his van. Fall is a good time to hold reunions. Most family members can attend because their crops have already been harvested.

Tomorrow I'm going to go visit with Miriam at her home. She is going to show me how to put a crazy patch quilt together. She is also going to show me some of the basic embroidery stitches. I'm interested in using some old scraps that I purchased at an auction.

*Rebecca*

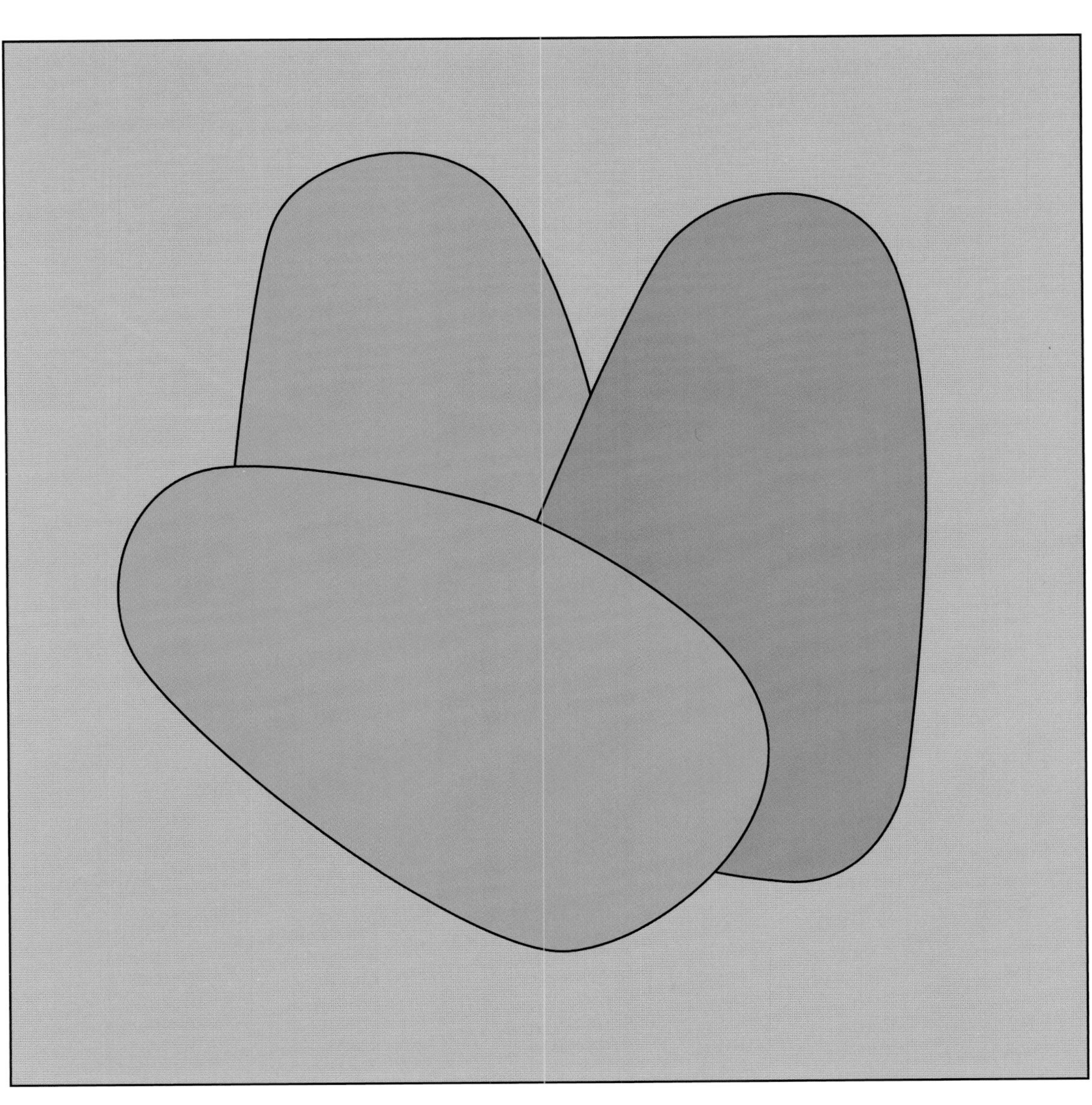

# 93. Tumbling Blocks

November 29

Dear Friends,

The weather is becoming much cooler lately. We have made sure that we have plenty of wood cut and stacked in the woodshed. Our wood box in our house needs to be filled constantly lately. Raymond is going to go with Daniel and Noah this weekend to a carriage auction to buy a sleigh because we are expecting such a cold winter.

Martha, I have helped our neighbor, Elva Kraybill, prepare breakfast for some English tourists that sometimes stay at her bed and breakfast. We usually served egg casserole, baked oatmeal and pecan cinnamon biscuits. The only real problem that she has is explaining to the tourists about taking photographs and explaining to them that her dishes and hand-embroidered linens are not for sale.

The girls are coming along well with their quilting and I have been teaching them how to hand piece the Tumbling Blocks pattern. I'm thinking about using cotton flannel for the batting this time, as I hear it is easier to stitch through and the thin layer of flannel provides more warmth.

Lavina

# 94. Neighbor's Bonfire

December 10

Dear Friends,

Our neighbor, Ben Zarger, had some of the neighbors over to ice skate on his pond. Some of the children went for sleigh rides while others sat around the bonfire and drank hot chocolate. Some of the older boys started a game of ice hockey. Everything seemed to be going well until Samuel Yoder went to a section of the pond where the ice was too thin and fell through. Some of the men ran to the barn and were able to get some rope to pull him out. He seemed fine. Leroy ran down the street to the phone booth, and soon an ambulance was there to take him to the hospital to check him out. We have heard that he spent the night at the hospital, but now has returned home.

Things seem to be going well on the farm. Our herd of dairy cows has now increased to over 200. Our whole family has learned to help with the morning and evening milking. We store our milk in the large steel containers and the milk companies usually pick them up every other day. Our district does not allow any milking machines or refrigerators like some of the other less conservative districts. We feel that we need to cling to the old ways and resist the new ways.

Edna

# 95. Fence Row

December 17

Dear Friends,

Tuesday started out to be like any other day. Little did we know what the night would bring. After evening prayers, Edith and the boys headed upstairs with their flashlights to get ready for bed. Timothy lit the gasoline lamps. All of a sudden, we heard a crash and the gasoline lamp fell and ignited Edith's bedcovers. The boys came running with her down the steps. Marvin tried to put the flames out, but the smoke was too thick.

The boys ran to get Marvin's brothers to help extinguish the blaze while one of his sisters-in-law ran down to the telephone booth. The fire engines did not arrive for about 10 minutes and in that time the house was a total loss. We were so thankful to God that we were all safe. We will be staying on the property, living with Marvin's family. The people in our district have all gathered to help us. They came bringing meals, clothing and household goods. They have scheduled a clean-up day for this coming Saturday. The following Saturday, we will start rebuilding our house.

Marvin's sisters presented each of our family members with a new quilt. Two of the quilts were Monkey Wrench patterns, which they presented to Timothy and Joseph. Martin and I received a Center-Diamond quilt and Edith received a Lone Star quilt. They even presented little Wilma with a baby quilt, using the Fence Row pattern.

*Frieda*

December 28

Dear Friends,

We celebrated Christmas at my sister's home. I presented the children with new lunch pails and more wooden farm animals to go with their barns. The twins, Karen and Emery, carried their lunch pails around with the animals in them. The children presented me with a hand-embroidered tea towel that one of my sisters had made.

We're all meeting at my sister's tomorrow to work on a special quilt for a fund-raiser to help little Samuel Garber because he recently had a stay at the hospital with pneumonia. He has just returned home and is doing very well. He is the 12th child of Jonas and Martha Garber.

Lavern

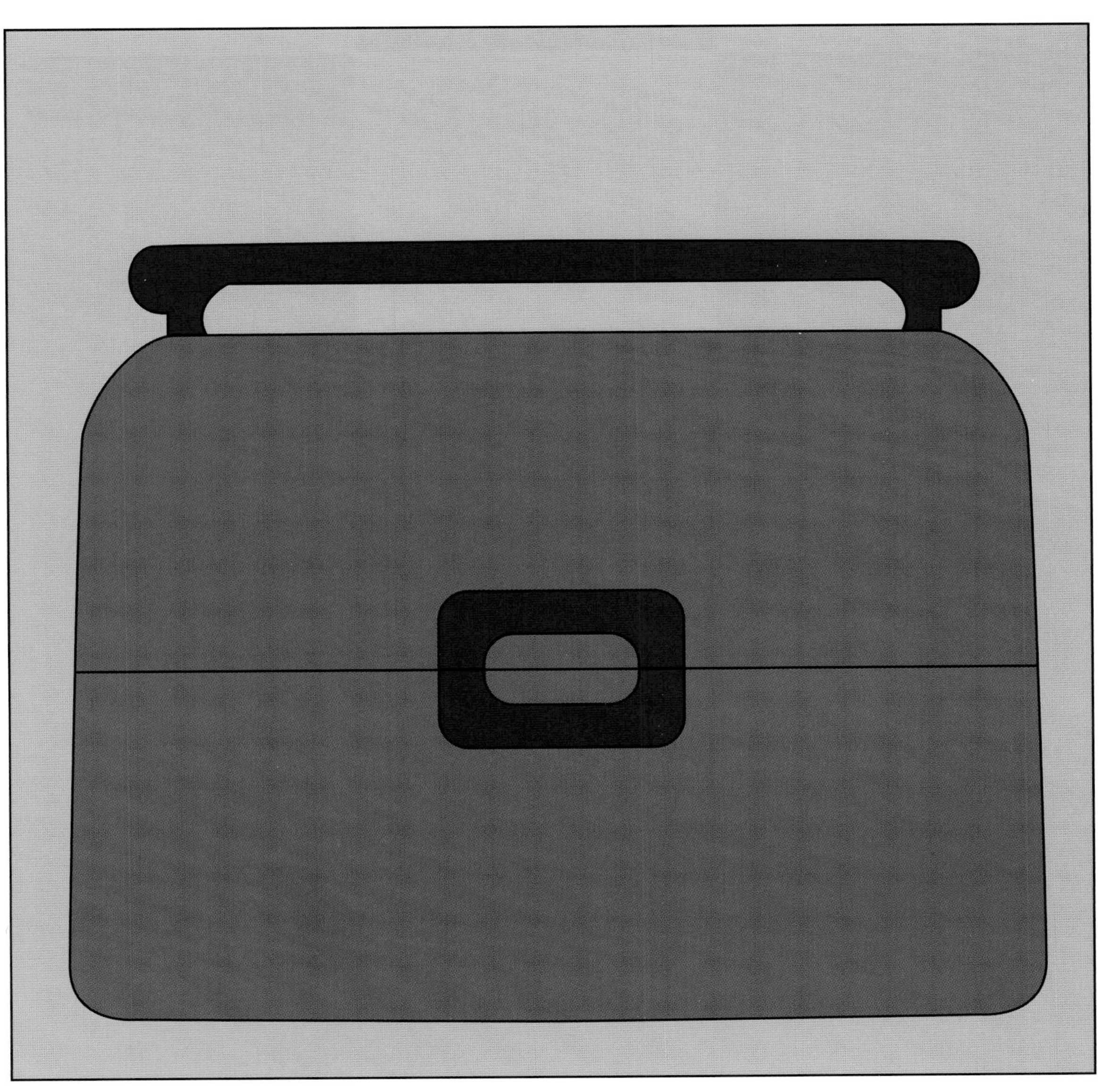

# 97. Nine-Patch

January 5

Dear Friends,

On Monday we ventured out in the winter weather and went to a quilting at Sarah Whetstone's home. We have decided to work on a couple of quilts for relief aid. We all had to bring 6" blocks using the simple Nine-Patch pattern. We had the tops together in no time and were soon seated around the frame catching up on each other's lives. Sarah's mother provided us with a hot lunch of meat loaf and roasted potatoes. She served schnitz pie for dessert, and the dried apples in the pie were very sweet. She made peanut butter cookies for the children. She does not like to quilt, but she likes to cook very much.

When we were done, she sat in her rocking chair and shared stories about her childhood with the children. They sat there so attentively and really enjoyed her stories. We enjoyed them as much as the children did. John spent the night retelling the stories to his brothers and sisters.

Mary and Faye are both going to be working on a whole-cloth quilt. They would like to learn a little bit more about how to quilt feathers, simple leaves and vines. They have been working mostly on straight line quilting. Their stitches seem to be getting smaller with every quilt that they do.

*Ida*

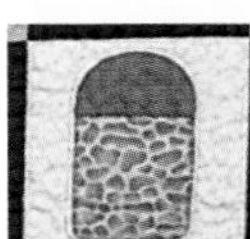

# 98. Broken Silo

January 15

Dear Friends,

Yesterday some of the women from our church district gathered at my home for a candymaking frolic. We spent the day making fudge, peanut brittle and taffy to sell along with some baked goods at a local store on Saturday. The money that we will raise from the sale will be given to Frieda's family to help them rebuild their home after the fire. A good time was had by all. Even the children were very eager to help.

Freeman also had a busy day yesterday. He was having trouble with the silo loader and had to feed all the cows and livestock by hand. When one of the husbands came to pick up his wife after the candymaking, he was able to help Freeman fix the silo loader. The bishop in our district does allow the farmers to use tractors and silo loaders to increase the farmers' productivity. One farmer was shunned last month because he went against the rules and started using rubber wheels on his tractor. This is forbidden in our district and he soon repented and returned to using steel wheels.

Tonight we're having the David Yoder family for dinner. They have just moved into our district after serving as missionaries in Haiti. They have three sets of twins in their family of seven children.

Regina

# 99. Spider Web

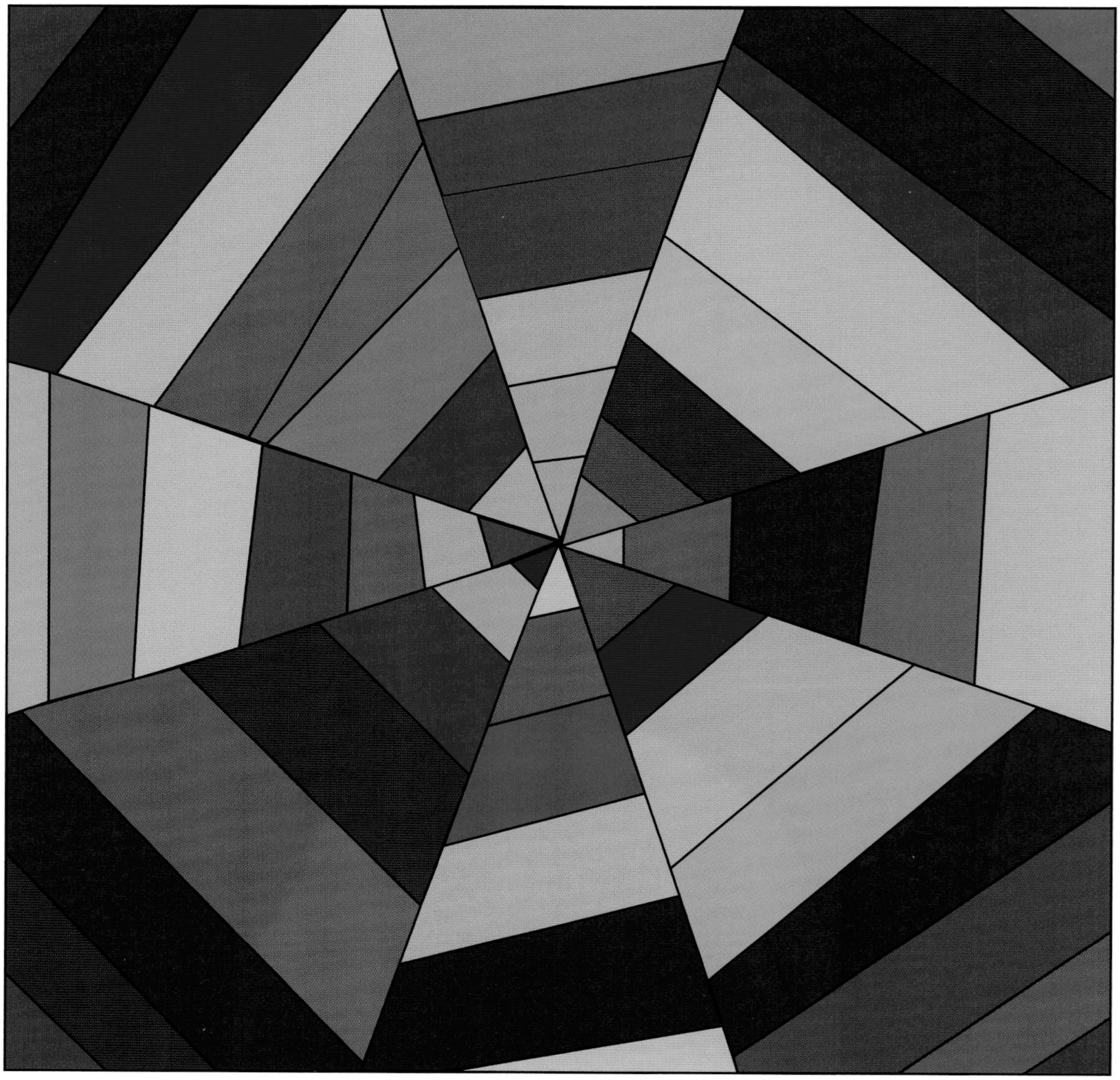

January 21

Dear Friends,

I have been piecing together a Spider Web quilt to use up a lot of my scraps from my scrap bag. Daniel's sisters have also donated many scraps from their scrap bags, so this definitely will be a family quilt, containing scraps from all of us. The children are doing well and little Charlene has been such a joy to our family.

I am so glad that we have kept in touch over the years through our circle letter. I talked to my neighbor, Susie Glick, about our circle letter and she was telling me that she has kept in contact with the girls from her eighth grade class through a circle letter, too. She said this was the first year that the circle was broken because one of the members died from cancer. They have never exchanged quilt blocks, but do exchange recipes.

Speaking of recipes, it is time to get my chores done and get our breakfast ready. Today for breakfast we are going to have pancakes topped with maple syrup and baked oatmeal soaked in warm milk. Pancakes are the boys' favorite. I think they could eat them every day and never get tired of them.

Miriam

# 100. Ice Skates

January 29

Dear Friends,

The weather has been unusually cold and we have been spending a lot of time in the kitchen. Since the kitchen is the only heated room in our home, we are thankful that the sale of baked goods to the local grocers is continuing to do well. We have not been selling as many baked goods to the English customers at our home because of the cold weather.

Our family went down to Delbert Eicher's pond to ice skate last night. All of the families from our church district were invited. The men used some metal barrels cut in half to make a couple of grills. They came in handy not only for warmth, but for roasting marshmallows and keeping the hot chocolate warm. Delbert gave some of the smaller children sleigh rides. It was a wonderful evening had by all and we ended the night singing our favorite hymns.

I have finished quilting my One-Patch quilt using the salesman's swatches. I quilted the top using an old pumpkin seed stencil that my great-grandmother had used on many of her quilts. Martha and Lena have been working the last few nights putting on the binding.

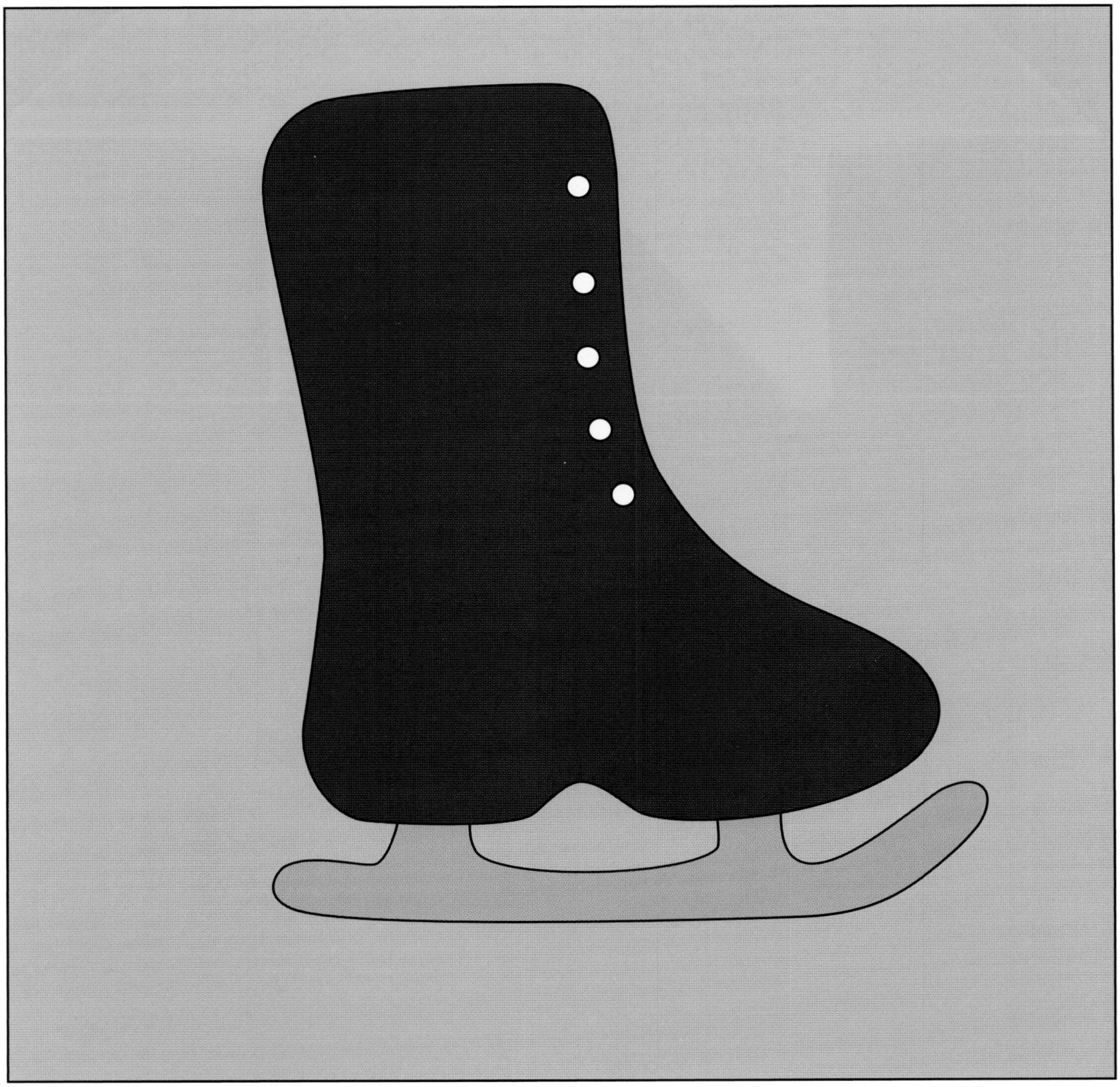

# 101. Ohio Star

February 6

Dear Friends,

It seems like we're having much better weather in Pennsylvania than most of you are. It has been sort of a mild winter with less snowfall than usual. Roy and the children are doing very well. Roy has been in the blacksmith shop getting the farm equipment ready for the coming spring. The children had a school project of making farm dioramas out of shoeboxes this week.

Most families in our district are butchering their livestock to fill their shelves with canned beef and pork. Roy worked last week at Roman Garber's home with another family to get the butchering done for the winter. The women enjoyed getting together and Sarah Schlabach presented each of us two quilters with 15 Ohio Star blocks. They were old blocks that she received from her grandmother. Sarah has never quilted, so we're going to surprise her and put them together in a quilt for her family.

February 15

Dear Friends,

Everything seems to be going well here. As I had told you last time, one of my English neighbors approached us about preparing meals for some tourists. We tried it once, but it became too intrusive to our familly and our bishop paid us a visit and reminded us about the verse, 2 Corinthians 6:14. We're happy with the decision that we have made.

Rachel came to visit today with her children and we had a nice visit baking pretzels. The smaller children really enjoyed rolling out the dough. Soon lunch was finished, as well as most of the fresh pretzels. As the older children cleaned up the dishes and played with the younger children, Rachel and I had some time to sit at the frame and visit. I have started hand piecing a double pinwheel quilt while I have a nine-patch in my frame.

Tomorrow we're going to have a quilting at Vesta Kaffmans' home. Her brother-in-law, John Chupp, had to have open heart surgery and the quilt will be used for a fund-raiser to help pay for his numerous hospital bills.

*Martha*

# 103. Crazy Patches

February 23

Dear Friends,

Today I spent the morning at Raymond Garber's home. His wife has been going through cancer treatments and is not up to doing all the housework. There were 10 women there from our church district to wash her windows, walls and floors. We also prepared some meals for them for the upcoming week. With so many helping, the work was done in no time.

When I returned home, I found some time in the afternoon to work on my crazy patch quilt that Miriam has been helping me with. I have really enjoyed putting together the quilt and doing the embroidery work. My grandmother really enjoys embroidery also, so I put together 30 extra blocks that she could embroider. She no longer quilts, but loves to sit on the porch and embroider while she watches the children play in the yard.

Lyle and the children are doing well. The weather is warming up some here, so soon we will be working in the fields and gardens. Wednesday is our sister's gathering and we're going to be meeting at Ada Kauffman's home to work on a quilt for one of my nieces for her upcoming wedding.

*Rebecca*

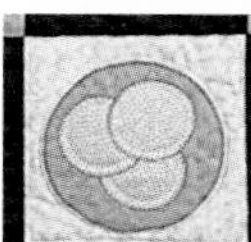

# 104. Pancake Supper

March 1

Dear Friends,

Spring is almost here, the sun is shining and all the snow has melted away. The weather has been unpredictable the last few weeks. One day it is snowing with the next day spring-like. Some farmers have been seen out in their fields plowing already. I cannot wait to get busy planting fresh vegetables again.

Monday we had a pancake supper at the school as a fund-raiser for Samuel Raber. He had a bout with pneumonia last week and had to stay in the hospital for four days. We also held a quilting on Tuesday and Wednesday at Edith Herschbergers' to make two quilts. We are going to hold a raffle at a local store to help raise money to pay his hospital bills. He is feeling much better now. I have enclosed his address for a card and money shower. His wife just gave birth to triplets last month, so any money you can give would be appreciated. They have so many bills to pay.

Raymond kept very busy working in his buggy and harness shop this winter. He has had a lot more English customers come to him to do their work. The children are all doing well. Thursday we spent part of the afternoon at school because the children had a multiplication tables bee. The scholars all rattled off their multiplication tables. After the bee, the families had a light lunch and then returned home.

Lavina

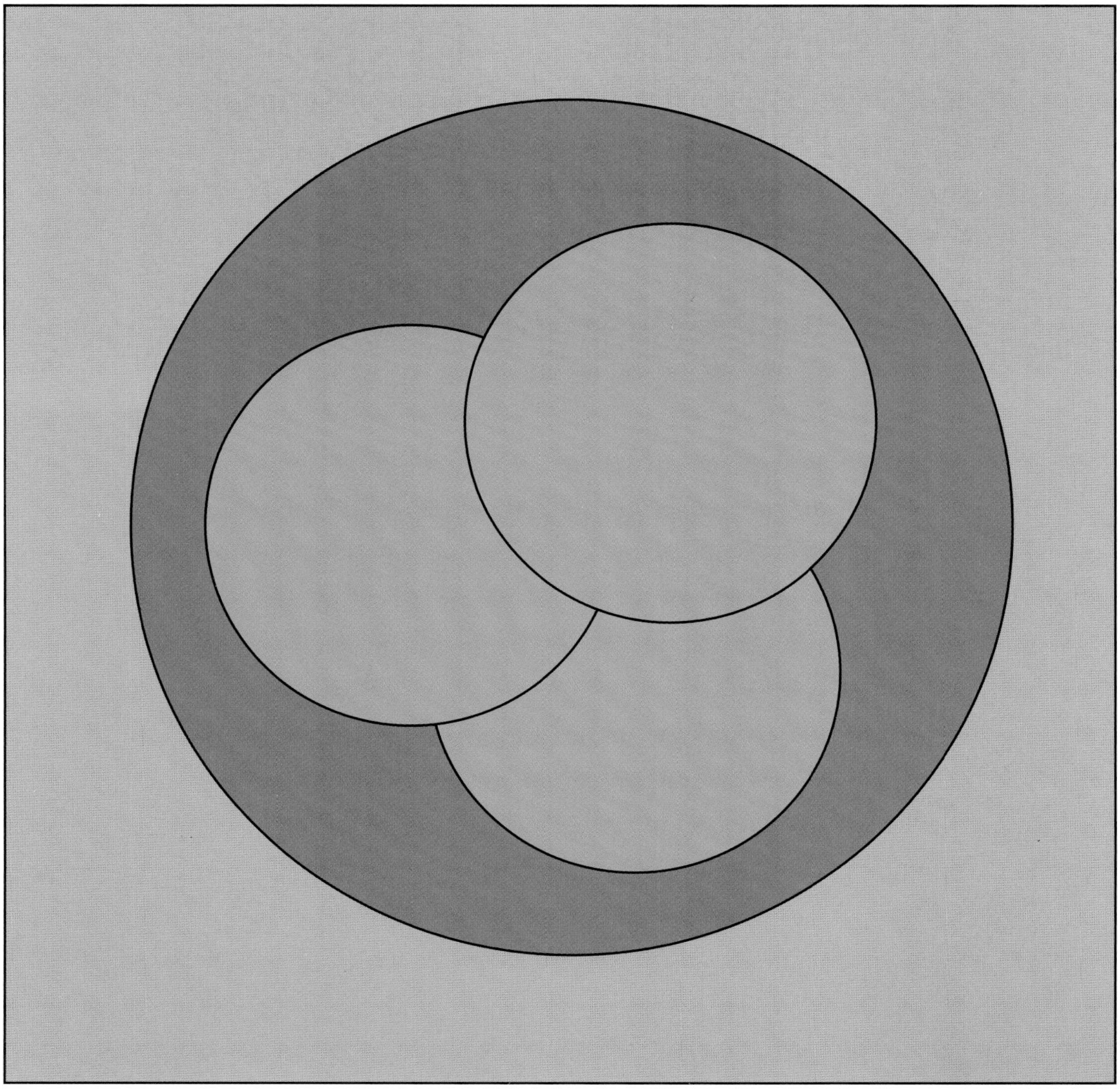

# 105. Birdhouse

March 9

Dear Friends,

The day started out very busy with a milk truck arriving at 5:00 this morning. The milk truck arrives every other day on our farm. As the boys get older, Leroy has been adding more dairy cows to our herd. Next month we are going to have a barn raising to build another barn for more dairy cows. Naomi is really excited because she figures that we will have to get more kittens to live in the barn as mousers.

As soon as breakfast was done and the children were off to school, I hung the laundry. I did notice that there are a lot more birds in the area already building nests in our bird houses. I had a lot of mending to do in the afternoon, as it was time to get some of the spring clothing out. I spent some time lowering the hems of the girls' dresses and mending some of the boys' pants.

I have a Nine-Patch quilt in my frame that I am making for a mission relief sale. My sisters are coming over tomorrow to help me finish quilting it. I enjoyed your letters, but it is now time to get back to my chores.

March 15

Dear Friends,

Our family was blessed with a little boy on February 26th named Jake, after his grandfather. Wilma is now walking and enjoys babbling to Jake. Edith is such a big help to me in the kitchen and with the children, even though she is only 6 years old. The boys are keeping busy helping Marvin get the fields ready for planting.

Today when I went down to the cellar, I made a list of what was left and what we really need to plant this year. I dusted off all the shelves and jars and arranged them alphabetically so they would be easier for the children to find. I brought up some pickled vegetables and canned pork for supper. So many people were so generous to us after the fire that the new cellar is full.

Our neighbors and our church district came together to help us after the fire and I was amazed at how fast the house went up, even in the middle of winter. We're all doing well and we are thankful to God for all the blessings we have received.

*Frieda*

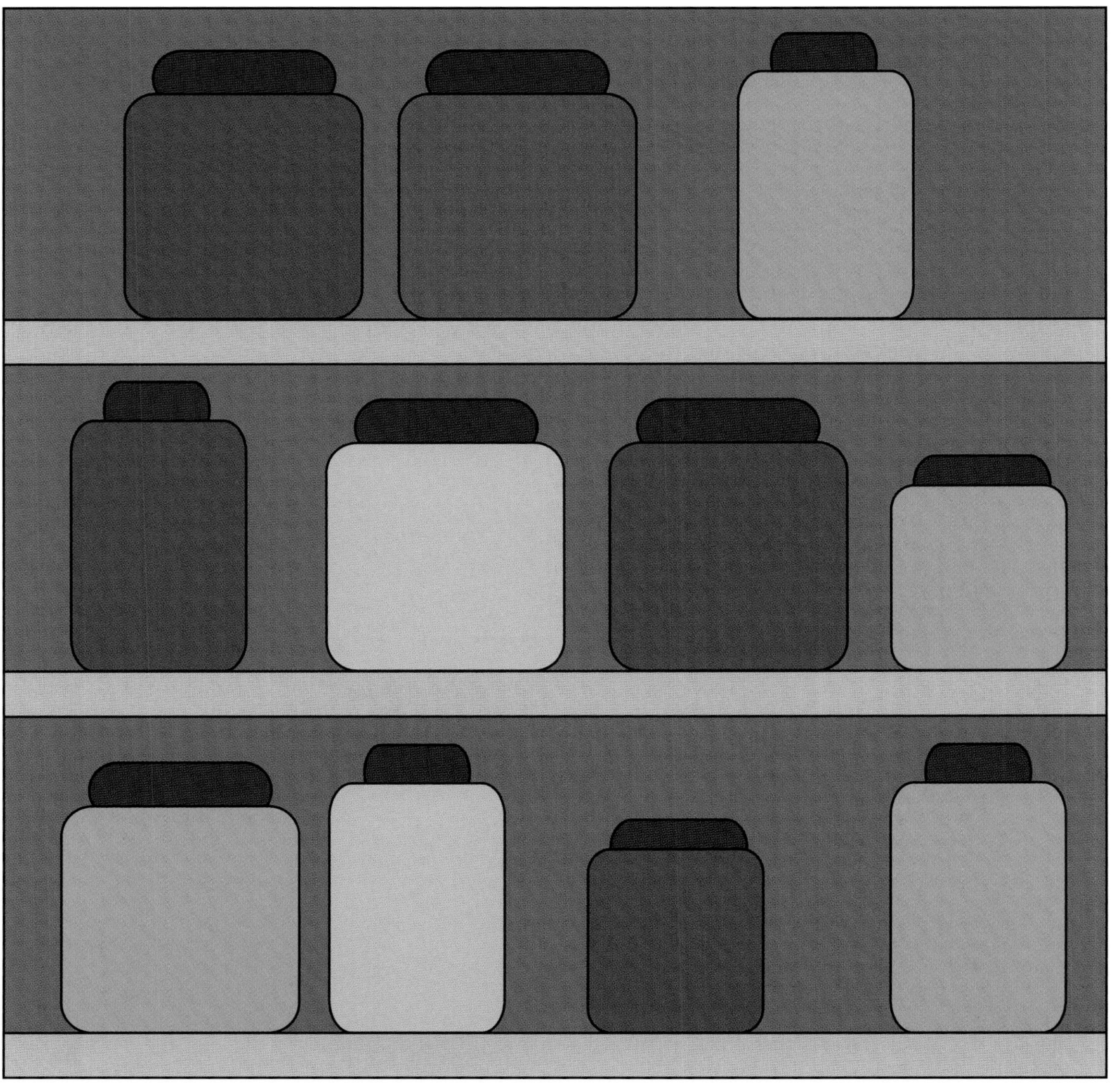

# 107. Nine-Patches Between Bars

March 28

Dear Friends,

A lot has happened in this past month. As most of you know, I married Jonas Miller last week. His wife passed away from cancer a year ago and left him to take care of their only child, Wayne, who is three years old. We have been in the process of moving into our new home which is in our same district. I have enclosed my new address. He has a very large family and his parents are living in the Dawdy House.

His first wife ran a dry goods store out of their home. Jonas has left it up to me whether I want to continue to do so or not. I am not sure how it will go, but I am going to try it. His wife left a Nine-Patch quilt in the frame. The nine patches are set on a point and set between bars. I asked Jonas if I could finish it and put it away for Wayne someday. He thought that was a good idea.

I still am planning on holding our quilting reunion at our home this August.

Lavern

# 108. Geese

April 6

Dear Friends,

Spring is here and we are enjoying the busyness this season brings. The children were outside picking dandelions today, so we will be having dandelion greens in our salad. Abe has been busy working to get the fields ready. It seems like he is plowing from morning until night.

The children have really enjoyed the visiting geese this season. For some reason, we have these two geese that showed up about a month ago and have not left. They seem to be following the children around most of the day and are becoming family pets. The only one who does not seem to enjoy their visit is our dog. He stays as far away from them as he can.

Mary has met an English girl when she helps out at the local bakery. She has asked if she would be allowed to spend the night at her home. Abe has told her no. He feels very strongly about 2 Corinthians 6:14.

*Ida*

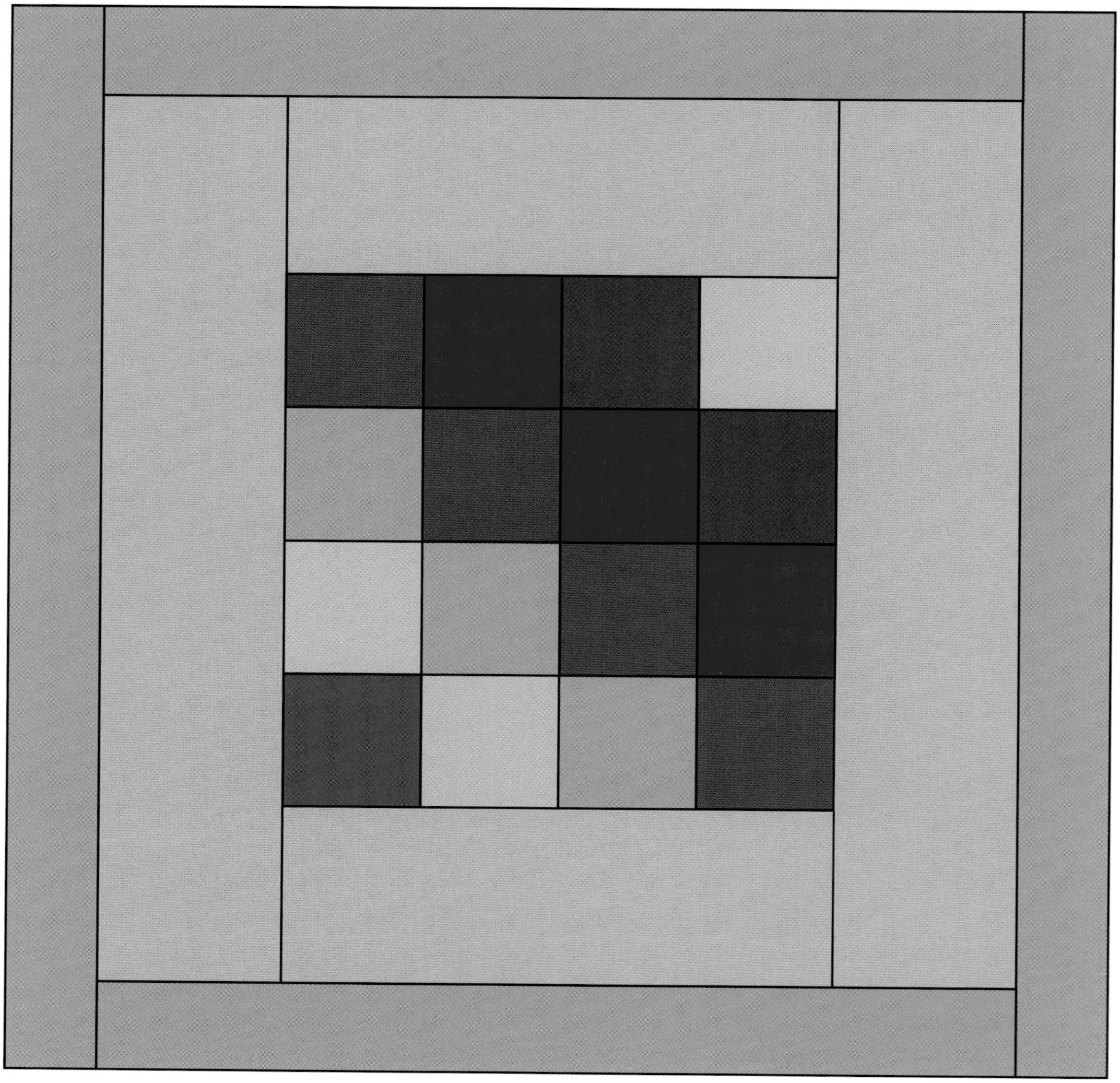

# 109. One-Patch

April 15

Dear Friends,

We're all doing well down here in Ohio. Freeman and his workers have been very busy working in the alfalfa field. He has hired three additional Amish neighbors to help on the farm this season. We are expecting a high yield because we have had such a rainy spring so far. The older boys will only be attending school for half-days the last two weeks so they can help out more on the farm.

We had a meeting at the school today during lunch to see what the children would like to do for their school picnic and trip. It was decided that they will be taking a trip to a local zoo and on the way home, we will be stopping to drop off some quilts at a local nursing home. Some of us mothers have been meeting the last few weeks and have put together about 20 tops using large squares of fabric. The mothers took turns coming to school at lunch time and the children tied the comforters together.

I am enclosing a small piece of muslin for you all to sign for my next block. You will have to wait until the next letter to see what pattern I'm going to use. I just put a Center-Diamond quilt in my frame. I am enjoying quilting the large feathers in the border. Martha would rather do the crosshatching behind the feathers. Well, it is time to get back to work.

*Regina*

# 110. Watering Can

April 26

Dear Friends,

Our family is very good and have just returned from the school picnic. The children are glad that school is out for the summer. Katie could not wait to take off her school dress and put on her work dress and go out to the chicken coop. The boys are all outside now helping Daniel with the evening chores. The boys each have their own watering can and are watering the raspberry and strawberry plants. It is quiet and Charlene is taking a nap before supper, so I thought it would be a good time to sit down and answer our circle letter.

Some of you may know Aden Stutzman. He lives down our street and has left his church to go to another church. The bishop has reprimanded him for attending another church and he was asked to change his ways and come back and ask for repentance. Our children are very good friends with their children and it will be very hard if there is a shunning . We are praying that he will change his ways.

I have taken Rebecca's crazy patch block and I'm going to do a whole quilt top using that pattern. I have learned so many stitches from Daniel's sisters, and I know it will be very helpful when I start the hand embroidery.

Miriam

# 111. Teacher's Bar Quilt

May 7

Dear Friends,

It is so good to have the school year finished and have the children home. The last few weeks were very busy with all of the projects for the end of the school year. We spent two days at Fannie Miller's home working on a bar quilt for the children's teacher, Martha Zargar. She is to marry Marvin Herschberger next week and will be retiring. Our end-of-the-year school picnic was a good time for all with 95 in attendance. On Saturday, some of the families were at the school with the children putting things away until fall.

The children are all busy doing their chores and Samuel's mother is in the kitchen baking some fresh pies. Today was laundry day and the most peculiar thing happened. A carload of English tourists stopped and asked if they could buy some of my dresses that were hanging on the line. After I said no, they asked if I had any quilts for sale. They soon left and then I noticed that they stopped at the neighbor's house. I know some of us in our community run businesses out of our homes, but I would think the English would not stop unless there were signs posted.

This summer will be a busy time, so I put away my quilt frame until September. Over the summer I am planning on hand piecing a Grandmother's Flower Garden quilt.

*Rachel*

May 15

Dear Friends,

The weather here in Pennsylvania has been in the 70s with just enough rain. The crops seem to be doing very well and it looks like I will be canning a lot of strawberry and raspberry jam in the next couple of weeks. The children are doing well. Clara and Katie seem to miss school, but William says he would rather stay home and work on the farm with Roy any day.

We're going to be having church at our home on Sunday. Some women are coming over today to help with the cleaning and cooking. I have a simple menu planned for lunch, so with all the help it will go very easily. Clara and Katie have spent the morning churning the butter and I already have the jellies and peanut butter spreads ready.

Remember how I told you that Sarah Schlabach gave Edith and me 15 Ohio Star blocks? Edith and I spent a day piecing them together and then had a quilting at her home. Sarah was so surprised and grateful when we presented her with the finished quilt. Since then, she has attended a few quiltings in our area and is now making quilts for her own family.

Lydiann

# 113. Double Pinwheels

May 27

Dear Friends,

Our family has been so blessed. On May 16th, we added two new boys to our family, named Galen and Ivan. It is very hard to tell the boys apart because they look so much alike. Our cellar is well stocked with canned goods from all of our neighbors and families who have been so generous.

Eli has hired Mattie Mast to help me out this summer. She is the daughter of Delbert and Elisabeth. She seems to be a very good worker and keeps very busy. Barbara follows her most of the day, trying to help her with her chores. The first week she was here, she worked on the sewing machine late at night and put together two Double Pinwheel tops for each of the boys. She is now hand quilting them. Her mother does a lot of quilting for some English customers and she helps her mother doing most of the machine piecing. She is a hard worker.

June 6

Dear Friends,

Our family had an exciting day last Saturday. We took the children to the local flea market and relief auction. We enjoyed looking at the quilts that were for sale. My sister and I made two for the auction. One of them was a Center Diamond quilt and the other was a Bar quilt. After the auction, we strolled down the aisles of the flea market and found two very good boxes of fabric scraps. Some of the pieces are already cut into triangles and we think it will make a nice Ocean Waves quilt. We were amazed that someone would want to sell such nice fabrics at only a dollar a box. Our husbands were able to purchase some used farm tools at a very good price. We bought the children some fresh hot pretzels and lemonade and then headed to my sister's for dinner.

Today, the block that I've enclosed with my letter is from the two quilts that we donated to the auction. I have been working on all the blocks we have exchanged and we have accumulated over a hundred of them. I am setting my blocks with a 1" lattice between them. I also have them in order like our circle letter and each row on my quilt will stand for each one of us. The children really enjoy seeing the blocks you send, as well as hearing the stories that go with them.

*Rebecca*

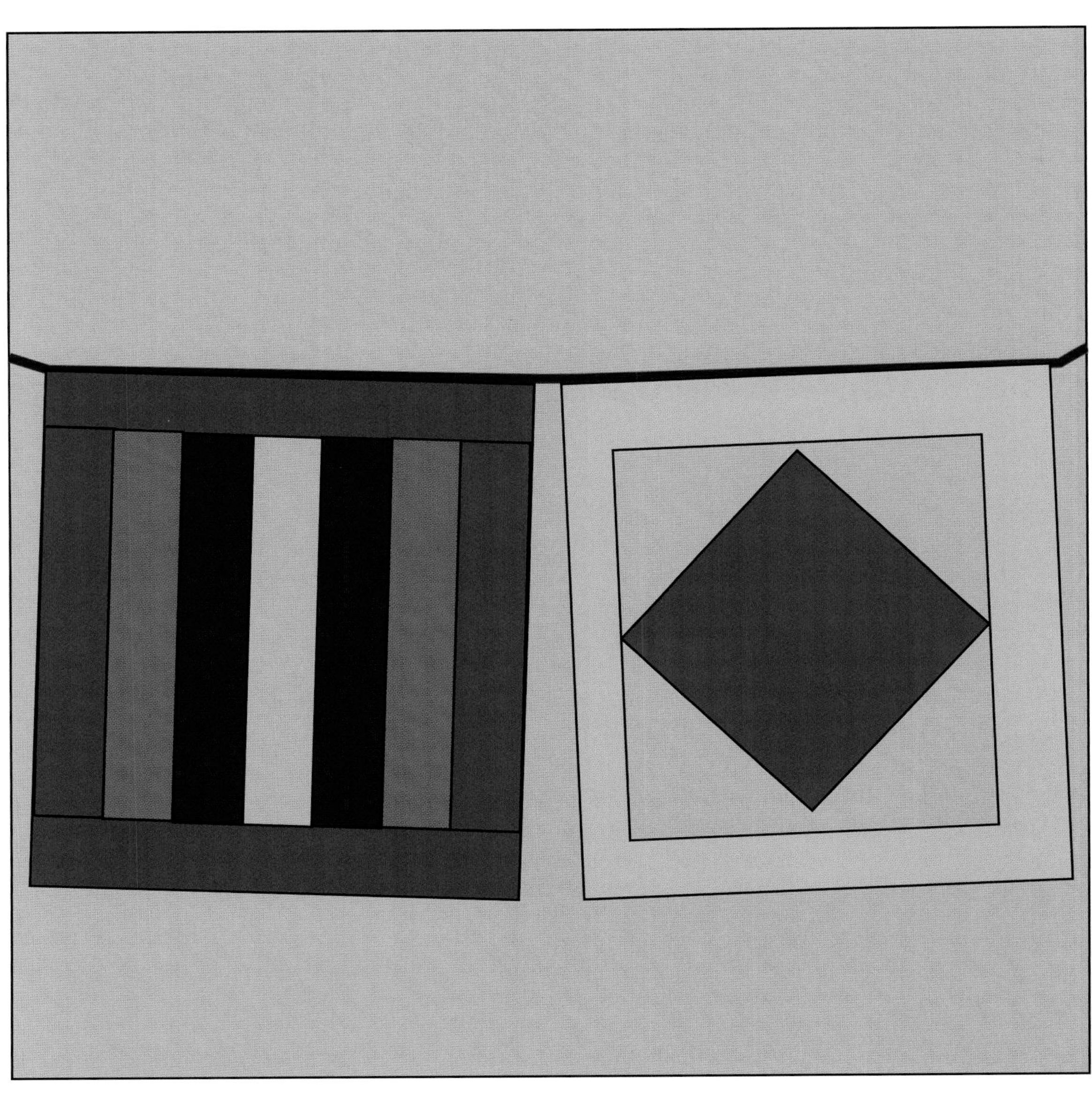

# 115. Flower Path

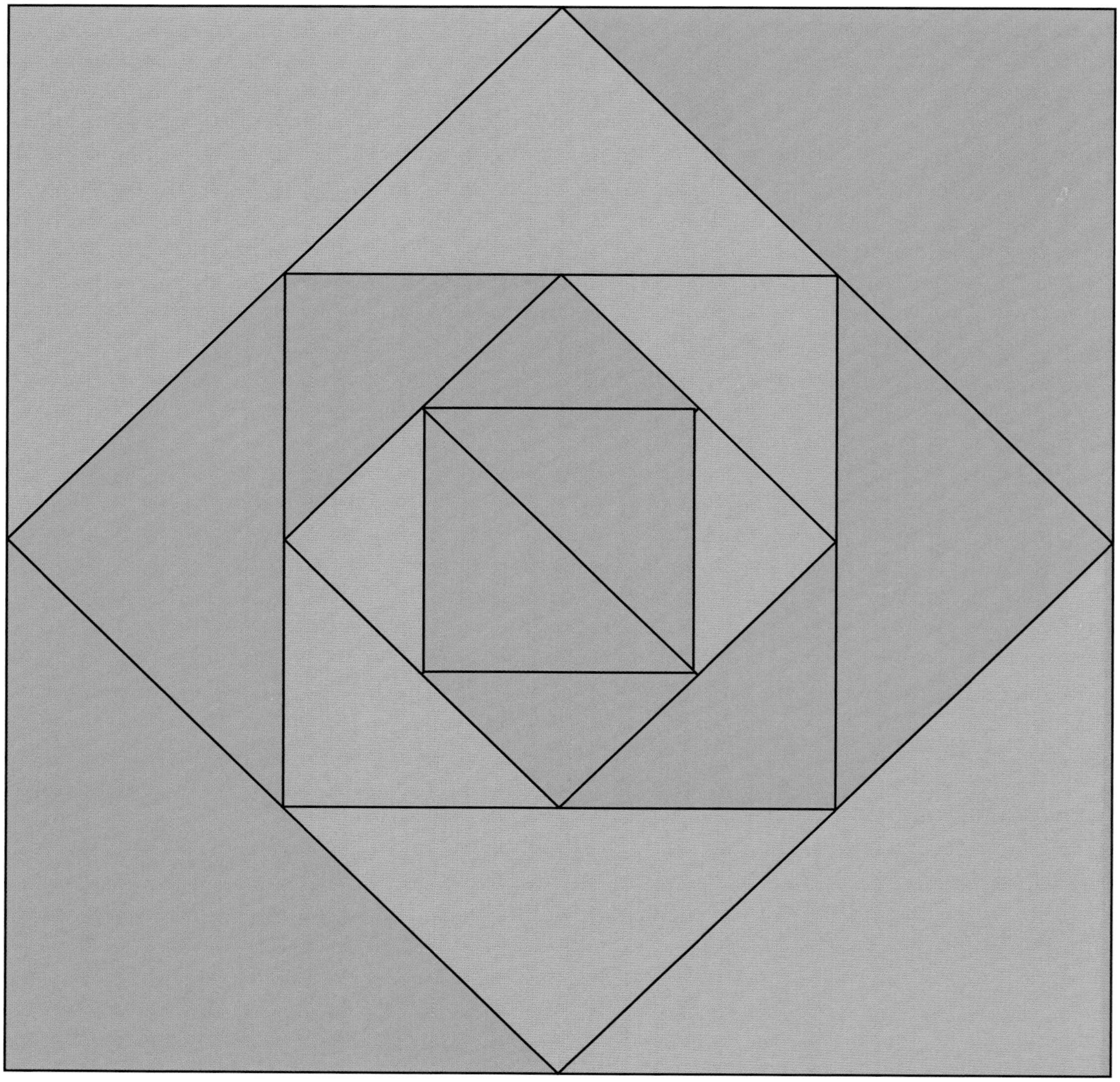

June 15

Dear Friends,

Rebecca, I did not realize that we have accumulated so many blocks. I have about 20 of them finished and work on them between my other projects. Things are going very well on the farm. We decided this year not to run our small vegetable stand. It seems like sometimes we have to sit there for hours before any customers arrive. We feel we spend too much time waiting for customers and that it could be better spent. We're working with the area grocer, who will be selling our vegetables. Raymond says the apple orchard will have a good yield this year and is looking at purchasing some of the neighbor's property to expand his trees.

The girls have been responsible for watering the vegetable garden and the flower garden. They have worn a path from the house to the gardens. We have decided, since they have been so responsible, that when the garden catalogs arrive in the fall, we're going to let them choose the flowers they want to plant. The boys all really like working on the farm. They really enjoy when the weather gets really hot because Raymond takes them down to the pond to cool off sometimes before supper.

Lavina

# 116. Roadside Stand

June 28

Dear Friends,

The barn raising went very well in April, with friends coming from all over to help. We even had some English neighbors volunteer. The dairy farming is going very well and Leroy has hired two of the neighbor's sons to help Melvin and Elvin with the milkings. Gideon is already a one year-old and is walking around. Naomi and Ruth are becoming more helpful every day.

Our roadside stand seems to do very well because we are on such a busy street. We have a lot of English customers that stop to buy our baked and canned goods. We only run our stand on the days when there is a lot of traffic for the flea market. There are three families in our neighborhood who run the stand, so it helps that we all take turns.

I have an Irish Chain quilt in my frame right now. It will be a wedding present for my sister, who is to marry next week. I also have been hand piecing some Tumbling Blocks together.

Edna

# 117. Double Nine-Patch

July 4

Dear Friends,

Everything here is going very well and our family is looking forward to the reunion at Lavern's home next month very much. We had a funeral on our farm last month, as Marvin's father passed away. He had a very large family and was a bishop of his district, so there were over 600 attending. He had liver cancer and had been going through chemotherapy treatments every week.

The children are all doing well. Little Jake is growing fast and little Wilma does not take her eyes off of him. The older boys are becoming very good at the farming chores and Edith has hand pieced her first quilt top using the Double Nine-Patch pattern that I have enclosed today. Yesterday when Marvin's sisters and I got together for our weekly quilting, we discussed how our daughters have really become interested in quilting at such a young age. Now instead of playing after lunch, most of them are hand piecing their blocks together.

Saturday our family is going to go visit Ida's family. Marvin is going to help Abe put up a fence for some new livestock. Lavern and I plan to combine and can some vegetables for our families.

*Frieda*

# 118. Making Apple Butter

July 9

Dear Friends,

We are looking forward to having you all to our new home for our reunion. I have chosen a Monkey Wrench quilt for us all to work on. The children are very excited and Jonas is looking forward to this new event.

We had a really nice time on Saturday at Jonas' brother's home. After spending most of Friday peeling apples, we arrived bright and early after morning chores to make some apple butter. The men fixed the fire and had a large kettle ready. Soon the apples were simmering and had to be stirred constantly. We all took a turn stirring the apple butter with large wooden paddles. It was soon time for afternoon lunch. We had fried chicken, mashed potatoes and gravy and a variety of fresh vegetables. This was all topped off by strawberry and raspberry pies. Later in the afternoon, the apple butter was done cooking. It was then divided between us and some of the local neighbors so we could take it home to can. All of us had a really nice time, with 116 in attendance.

Lavern

# 119. Square in a Square

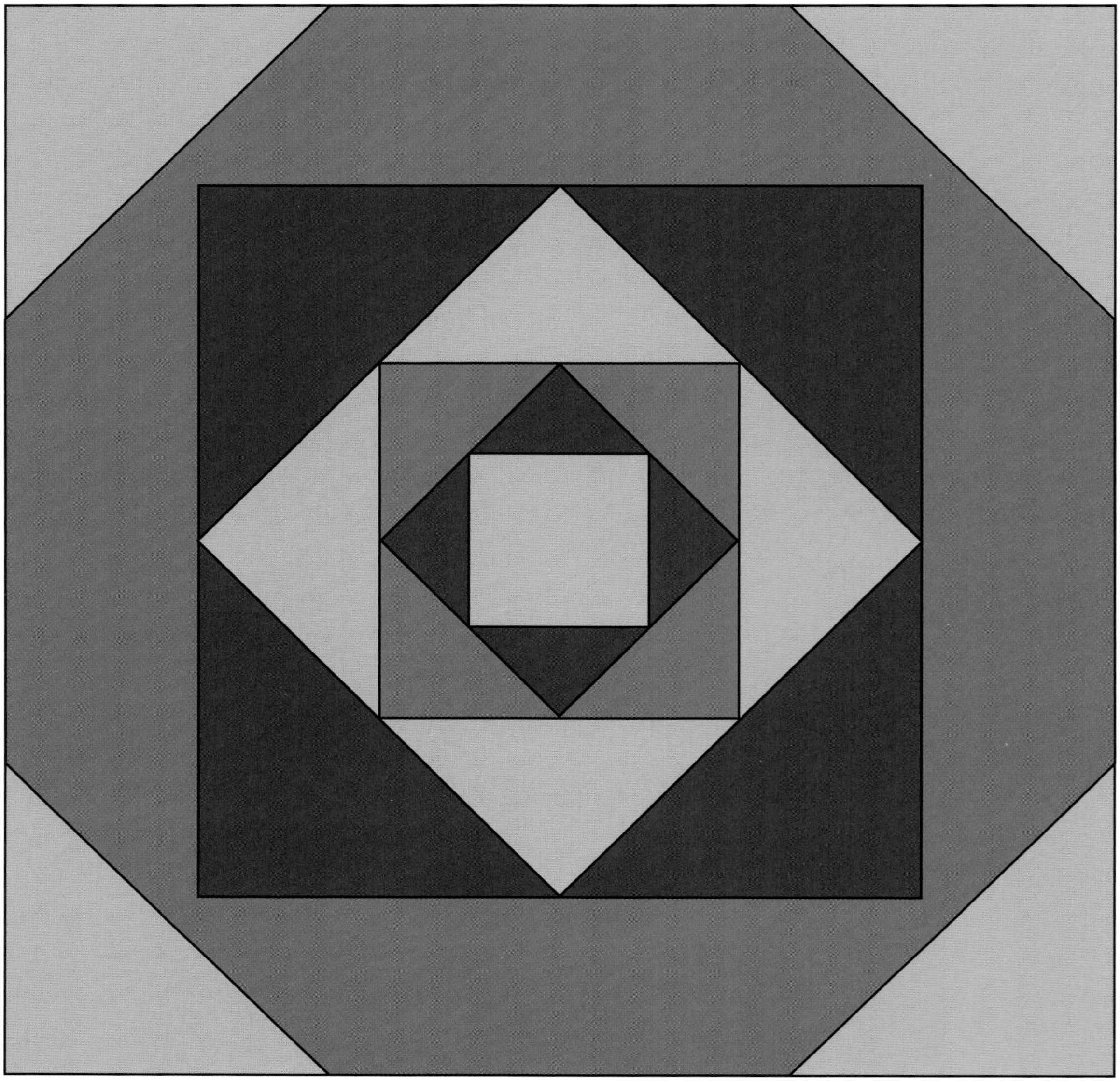

July 19

Dear Friends,

It is the typical hot July weather with temperatures well into the 90s. Joseph and the boys spent the morning washing the buggy before we headed off to a barn raising. Last week, Henry and Elona Lapp lost their barn during the storm. The lightning hit the barn and started the hay on fire. Their boys rode off on horseback to get some help from neighbors after the livestock was led out of the barn. The barn was a total loss, but no one was hurt.

Friends came from miles around to help put up the barn. There were over 100 in attendance. We cooked plenty of food and served the men lunch and supper. By the end of the day, most of the barn had taken its shape. They are going to meet again next Saturday to finish up the work that needs to be done.

I have just finished working on a Square in a Square quilt. I'm going to finish putting on the binding and take it with me next week for the Lapp family. They are also going to have two quilt frames set up for us to work on.

*Ida*

# 120. Signature Sunflowers

July 25

Dear Friends,

Our family is doing very well here in Ohio and looking forward to traveling to Indiana in two weeks for our reunion. We also have plans to stop and visit other relatives along the way. I know Freeman will enjoy the break, as we have had a very busy farming season this year. The hired Amish neighbors will be taking over the farming work for him.

I hope you all enjoy the block that I have enclosed. We have a lot of sunflowers in our garden this year and that is how I got the idea for you to sign the petals. There are 11 petals on my sunflower—one to represent each of us. The Center Diamond quilt that Martha and I have been quilting is finished and I will be bringing it to the reunion.

I'm going over to Erma Waglers' home this afternoon. We are having a canning frolic. She has had a couple of small strokes and has been unable to do her canning this year. The women from our church district are going to be cleaning up her vegetable garden and canning for her today. I'm sure that there will be other chores that need to be done.

*Regina*

# 121. Reunion

August 6

Dear Friends,

Lavern, we all had such a nice time at your home for our reunion. I cannot wait until we get to travel to Pennsylvania next year to Lydiann's home. The children are really looking forward to seeing Pennsylvania. I think that they enjoy the reunion as much as we do.

It was so good to see you and all of the quilting projects you have been working on. I am glad that we were able to finish Lavern's quilt. Rachel, you have kept up working on your blocks so well, and since this will be the last one for this quilt, I will leave it up to you to decide what we should do next. I think your idea of sending our favorite recipes for a while until we all can catch up on our blocks is a very good idea. I am amazed at how many of our children are working on the blocks. It is such a nice way for us to share the stories of our lives. I think the block that I am including is fitting because it reminds me of heading home from the reunion in our buggies. I'm so glad that we have kept in touch through our circle letter and I cannot wait for the next one to come in the mail.

Miriam

# The Projects

# 1930s Sampler

Finished size is approximately 28" x 35"

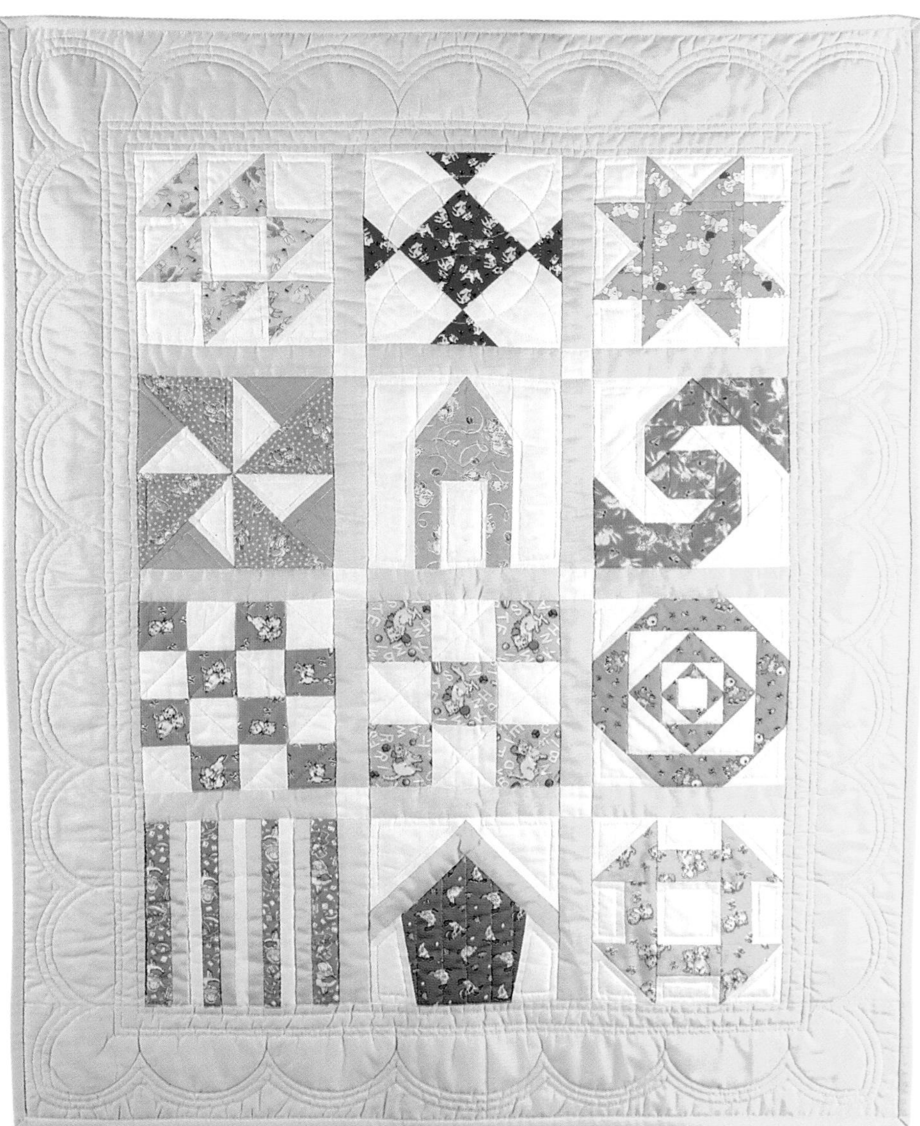

## Fabric requirements

- 1 yd. fabric for borders, lattice strips and binding
- ½ yd. fabric for background and cornerstones
- Various scraps used to make blocks
- 1 yd. fabric for backing

## Instructions

1. Assemble 12 of your favorite blocks.
2. Cut six cornerstones 1½" square and 17 lattice strips 1½" x 6½".
3. Assemble together (see the diagram on page 8). You will be assembling four rows of three blocks using only two lattice strips in each row. The connecting row will contain three lattice strips with two cornerstones.
4. Cut two border pieces 4½" x 27½" and add them to the sides of the blocks.
5. Cut two border pieces 4½" x 27½" and add them to the top and bottom of the blocks.

# Redwork Blocks of the Month

Finished size is approximately 29" x 37". Made by Barbara David.

## Fabric requirements

- 1 yd. fabric for borders, lattice strips and binding
- 1 yd. fabric for background, cornerstones and small border
- 1¼ yd. fabric for backing
- Red embroidery floss

## Instructions

1. Embroider the 12 blocks on 6½" background squares.
2. Cut six cornerstones 1½" square and cut 17 lattice strips 1½" x 6½".
3. Assemble together (see the diagram on page 8). You will be assembling four rows of three blocks using only two lattice strips in each row. The connecting row will contain three lattice strips with two cornerstones.
4. For the first border, cut two strips 1½" x 27½" and add them to the sides of the blocks. Cut two strips 1½" x 22½" and add them to the top and bottom of the blocks.
5. For the second border, cut two strips 1" x 29½" and add them to the sides of the first border. Then cut two strips 1" x 23½" and add them to the top and bottom of the quilt.
6. For the last border, cut two strips 3½" x 30½" and add them to the sides of the second border. Cut two strips 3½" x 29½" and add them to the top and bottom of the quilt.

# Table Topper

Finished size is approximately 20" x 41"

## Fabric requirements

- 1 yd. fabric for background, borders and binding
- ⅛ yd. fabric for lattice strips
- 1 fat eighth for cornerstones
- Various scraps used to make blocks
- 1 ¼ yd. fabric for the backing

## Instructions

1. Assemble four of your favorite blocks.
2. Cut 10 cornerstones 1½" square and cut 13 lattice strips 1½" x 6½".
3. Assemble together (see the diagram on page 8).
4. Cut two border pieces 6" x 8½" and add them to the sides of the blocks.
5. Cut two border pieces 6" x 41½" and add them to the sides to finish completing the border.

# Hailey's Baby Quilt

Finished size is approximately 33" x 47"

## Fabric requirements

- 1½ yd. fabric for background, binding and borders
- ¼ yd. fabric for lattice
- ⅛ yd. fabric for cornerstones
- Various scraps used to make blocks
- 1½ yd. fabric for backing

## Instructions

1. Assemble 15 of your favorite blocks.
2. Cut 24 cornerstones 1½" square and cut 38 lattice strips 1½" x 6½".
3. Assemble together (see the diagram on page 8). You will be assembling five rows of three blocks. The connecting rows will contain four cornerstones and three lattice strips.
4. Cut two border pieces 6" x 36½" and add them to the sides of the blocks.
5. Cut two border pieces 6" x 33½" and add them to the top and bottom of the blocks.

# Amish Wallhanging

Finished size is approximately 16" x 44"

## Fabric requirements

- ½ yd. fabric for binding, lattice strips and background color for blocks
- ½ yd. fabric for border
- 1 fat eighth for cornerstones
- Various scraps used to make blocks
- 1¼ yd. fabric for backing

## Instructions

1. Assemble five of your favorite blocks.
2. Cut 12 cornerstones 1½" square and cut 16 lattice strips 1½" x 6½".
3. Assemble together (see the diagram on page 8).
4. Cut two border pieces 4½" x 36½" and add them to the sides of the blocks.
5. Cut two border pieces 4½" x 16½" and add them to the sides to finish completing the border.

# Fabrics that Jane Stickle Would Have Used

Finished size is approximately 48" x 62". Jane A. Blakely Stickle made a quilt sampler in the 1860s. Her quilt has been such an inspiration to me and through that quilt I have met so many wonderful people. I chose the name of this quilt because if Jane Stickle were alive today, I feel she would have used Civil War reproduction fabrics to complete her Amish circle quilt.

## Fabric requirements

- 2 yd. fabric for border and binding
- ¾ yd. fabric for lattice strips
- 1½ yd. fabric for background and cornerstones
- Various fabrics used to make blocks
- 3½ yd. fabric for backing

## Instructions

1. Assemble 35 of your favorite blocks.
2. Cut 48 cornerstones 1½" square and cut 82 lattice strips 1½" x 6½".
3. Assemble together (see the diagram on page 8). Assemble seven rows of five blocks. The connecting rows will contain six cornerstones and five lattice strips.
4. Cut two border pieces 6½" x 36½" and add them to top and bottom of the blocks.
5. Cut two border pieces 6½" x 62½" and add them to the sides of the quilt.

# Bags and Aprons

Various sized bags and aprons

## Instructions

1. Purchase various bags and aprons at your local fabric and craft store.
2. Purchase ½ yard of fusible web.
3. Choose your favorite appliqué pattern and trace the pieces onto the fusible web. Follow the instructions that come with your fusible webbing.
4. It is not necessary to draw the pattern onto the bags or aprons, it is very easy to place the pieces onto your project just by eyeing where the piece goes.

# Gallery

These Amish circle quilts illustrate the variations that are possible using different fabrics and techniques. Each quilt is unique, beautiful and tells the story of "The Amish Circle Quilt."

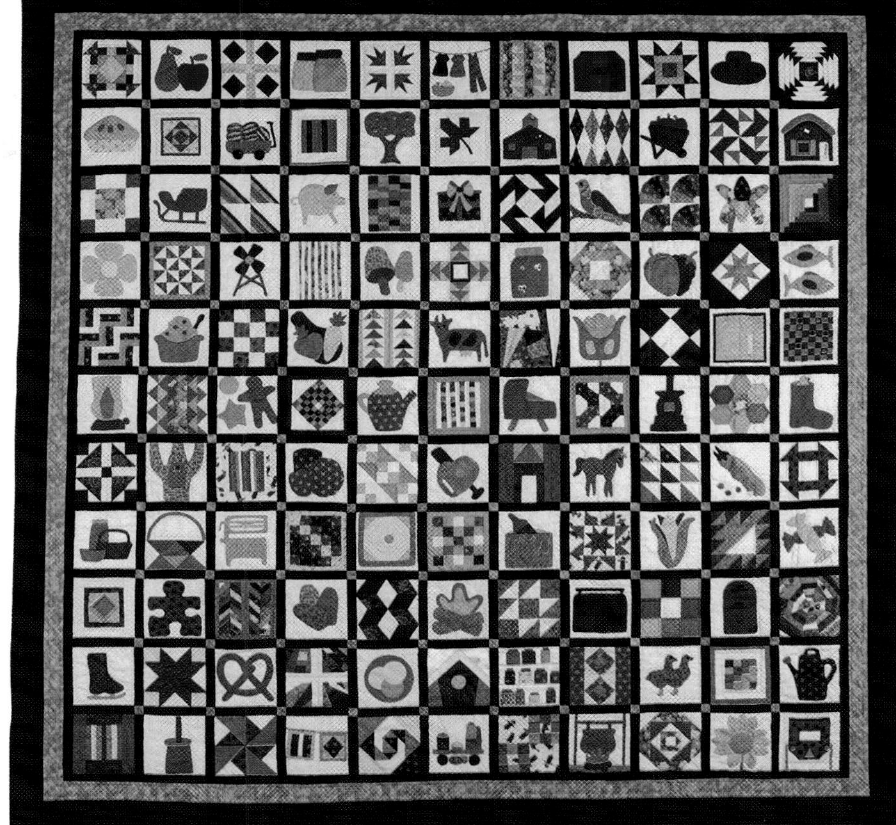

TOP:
*"Words and Pictures: My First Experience with Paper Piecing."*
Machine paper pieced, hand-appliquéd and quilted by Gretchen Houtman.
Finished size: 86" x 86"

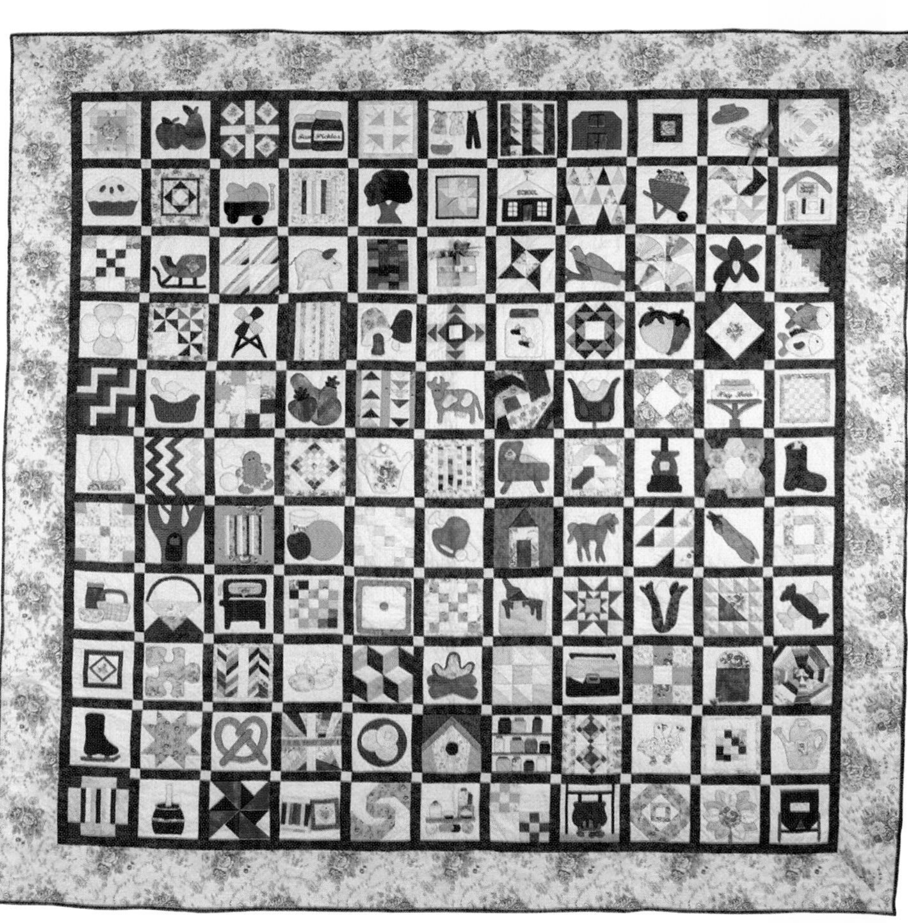

BOTTOM:
*"Circle Letter in the Garden."*
Pieced and quilted by Julie A. Dettloff.
Finished size: 92" x 92"

# Gallery

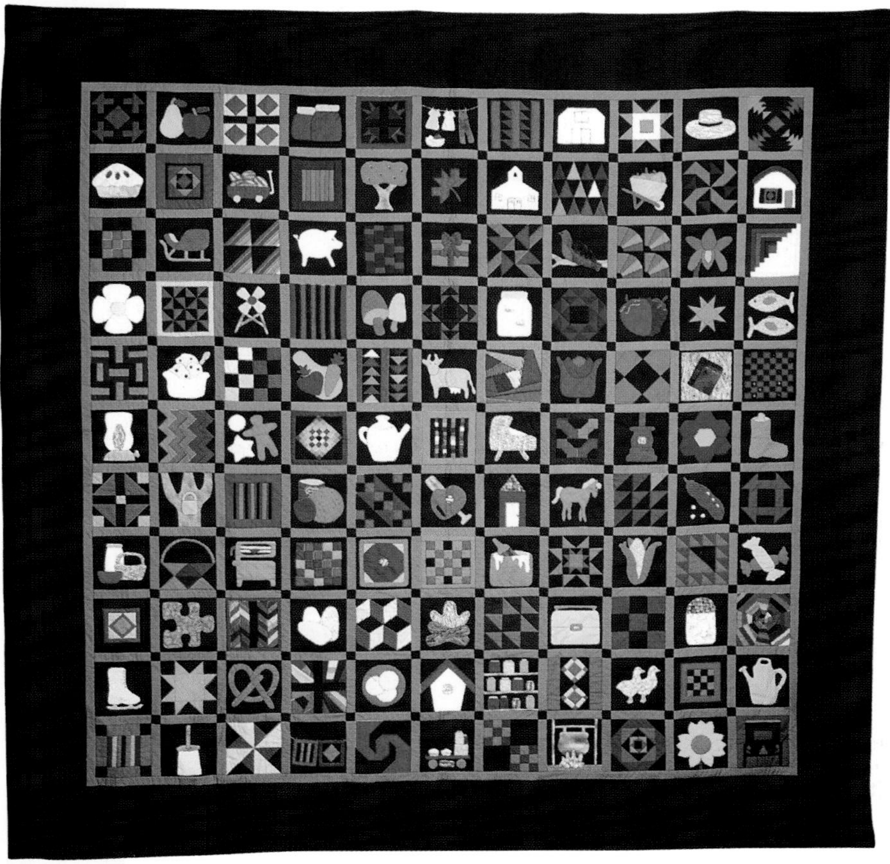

TOP:
*"Amish Circle Letter."*
Made by Barbara David.
Finished size: 95" x 95"

BOTTOM:
*"Rosemary's Amish Circle Letter."*
Made by Megan T. Harding.

# Gallery

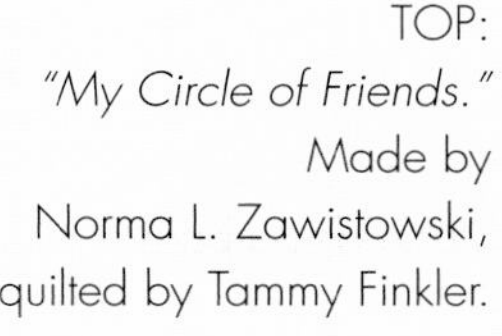

TOP:
*"My Circle of Friends."*
Made by
Norma L. Zawistowski,
quilted by Tammy Finkler.

BOTTOM:
*"Amish Circle Letter Quilt."*
Made by Sandy Ziebarth.

# Gallery

TOP:
*"Amish Circle Letter."*
Stitched and quilted
by Judi Anderson.
Finished size: 95" x 95"

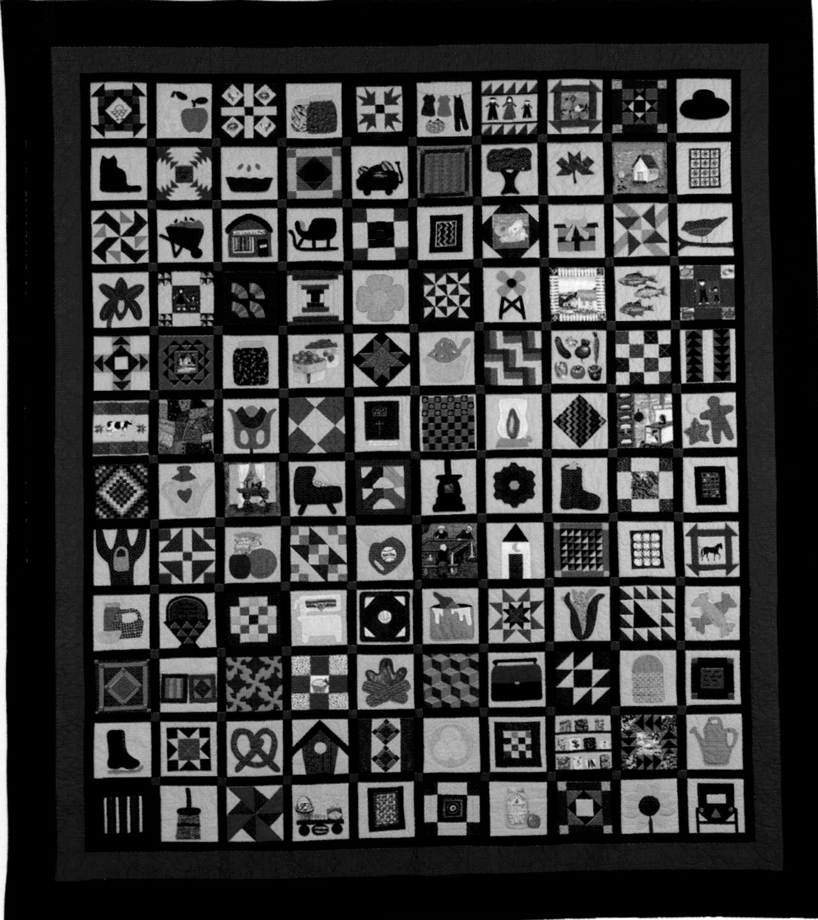

BOTTOM:
Made by
Marie McDonald,
machine quilted by
Tammy Finkler.
Finished size: 89" x 107"

# Gallery

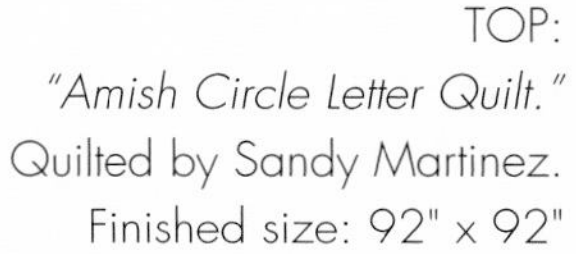

TOP:
*"Amish Circle Letter Quilt."*
Quilted by Sandy Martinez.
Finished size: 92" x 92"

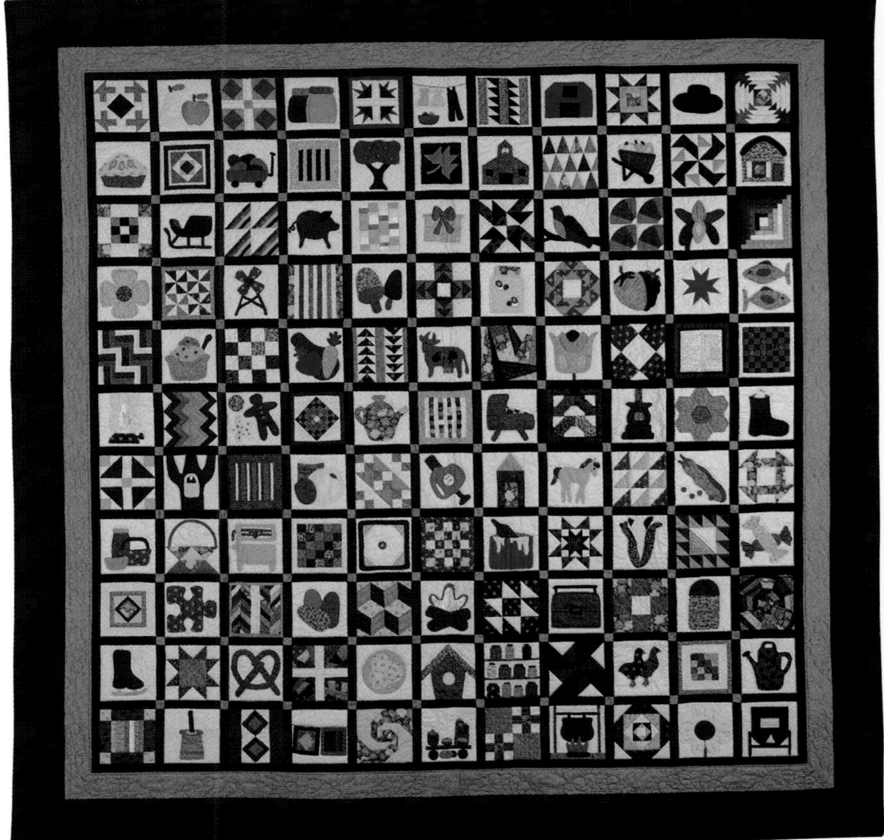

BOTTOM:
*"Amish Circle Letter."*
Made by Nancy Vida,
machine quilted by
Tammy Finkler.
Finished size: 92" x 92"

# About the Author

Rosemary Youngs began quilting in the 1980s after seeing a quilt at the State Fair. Her quilts have won numerous awards in local as well as major shows. Various books and magazines have also published some of her work. She has taught at local quilt shops and enjoys designing quilts that tell stories. She became especially interested in the Amish quilts and culture and, out of that interest, wrote the Amish circle letter in this book. Rosemary currently resides in Walker, Mich., with her family.

The quilters pictured are those who made the quilts in this book. First row: (from left to right) Rosemary Youngs, Megan Harding, Norma Zawistowski and Julie Dettloff. Second row: (from left to right) Nancy Vida, Barbara David, Sandy Martinez, Marie McDonald, Judi Anderson and Gretchen Houtman. Not pictured: Sandy Ziebarth.